The 25 Biblical Laws *of* Success

POWERFUL PRINCIPLES *to* TRANSFORM
YOUR CAREER *and* BUSINESS

WILLIAM DOUGLAS
AND RUBENS TEIXEIRA

BakerBooks
a division of Baker Publishing Group
Grand Rapids, Michigan

Published by Baker Books
a division of Baker Publishing Group
P.O. Box 6287, Grand Rapids, MI 49516-6287
www.bakerbooks.com

Printed in the United States of America

Library of Congress Cataloging-in-Publication Data
Names: Douglas, William, 1967– author.
Title: The 25 biblical laws of success : powerful principles to transform your career and business / William Douglas and Rubens Teixeira.
Other titles: Twenty-five biblical laws of success
Description: Grand Rapids : Baker Books, 2017. | Includes bibliographical references.
Identifiers: LCCN 2016045134 | ISBN 9780801019562 (pbk.)
Subjects: LCSH: Success—Religious aspects—Christianity. | Success—Biblical teaching. | Success in business.
Classification: LCC BV4598.3 .D68 2017 | DDC 248.4—dc23
LC record available at https://lccn.loc.gov/2016045134

18   19   20   21   22   23   7   6   5   4

For my parents,
for Nayara, my wife,
and for my kids, Luisa, Lucas, and Samuel
—William Douglas

For Paulo and Darcy,
Marta, and Renan
—Rubens Teixeira

Skill will bring success.

—Ecclesiastes 10:10

Be strong and very courageous. Be careful to obey all the law my servant Moses gave you; do not turn from it to the right or to the left, that you may be successful wherever you go. Keep this Book of the Law always on your lips; meditate on it day and night, so that you may be careful to do everything written in it. Then you will be prosperous and successful.

—Joshua 1:7–8

Contents

Introduction

What Does Professional Success Have to Do with the Bible?

The Bible is the greatest manual on professional success ever written. Although it is many centuries old, the Bible remains relevant today and shows you the path to success in the job market and in business management, regardless of whether you are religious or not. *The 25 Biblical Laws of Success* was written to share this knowledge with you.

The Bible's teachings have been confirmed by the experience of several respected professionals who built successful careers based on biblical laws, principles, and values. Professionals, managers, and employees can draw on biblical lessons to attain excellence, credibility, and professional achievements. The laws of the Bible are like keys: they work for everyone. If you use the right key, the safe opens. The laws you will learn in this book are keys that will open to you the doors to above-average results and success.

If you are asking yourself why so little is said about these professional lessons found in the Bible, the answer is simple: people usually see the Bible as a merely religious book. Many apply Scripture in a limited manner, obeying only its religious guidelines. Those not interested in religion completely miss out on important lessons that could boost their career. These oversights come at a high price, since both the former and the latter miss out on precious wisdom that could solve today's work challenges.

Professional success is a goal that is in part a direct consequence of your personal convictions and values. Success also results from a combination of attitudes, thoughts, and behaviors. Hard work alone will not guarantee lasting success. To achieve long-term professional success, you also need to develop characteristics such as discipline, willpower, resilience, intelligence, creativity, courage, determination, and self-control.

These values, all of which are expressed in the Bible, will be discussed in detail in this book. Of course, the Bible is not the only place where we can learn about values that are useful in life, but when we are talking about work and career, the Bible certainly has the greatest quantity and the best quality of advice.

The Laws of Success

Our world is governed by human laws. Whether a law is obeyed or infringed, there will be consequences. When people commit a crime, they go to jail; if people incorrectly pay a debt, they will have to make it right. ("Bad payers pay twice," goes an old Brazilian adage.) On the other hand, those who abide by the law, such as employers who respect labor legislation, have fewer problems and expenses. There is an upside to opting to act within the law. Everyone understands the force of human laws, such as civil, criminal, and labor laws.

Our world is also governed by natural laws. Everyone also understands the force of the laws of nature, such as the laws of physics and gravity. These natural laws affect us every day regardless of whether we like them or not.

What not everyone is aware of is the existence of yet another type of law: spiritual laws.

Most people think spiritual laws apply only to matters of religion, but there's more to them than that. Spiritual laws are immaterial laws that don't derive from human laws or the laws of nature. These spiritual laws are foundational life principles that can be split into religious laws (which are not the focus of this book) and nonreligious laws. For instance, when we say that those who do good receive good in return, or that envy generates bad energy, we are speaking of spiritual laws.

Man-made laws can often be broken without any resulting consequences. Someone who commits murder may not be found out or, due to a technicality, may escape conviction. Laws of nature work differently: they are inexorable and there will always be consequences. There is no getting away from them. For example, you may not be familiar with the law of gravity, or perhaps you don't agree with it, but if you jump from a building you'll splatter yourself on the ground below. When someone chooses to ignore such natural laws (as gravity) and thereby suffers its consequences, there is no moral issue involved. There is only cause and effect. People usually know how it works and they go along with it.

What many people don't know is that the laws of nature are not the only ones easily noticed. Just as the laws of physics, chemistry, and biology affect your everyday life—and just as accurately as the laws of mathematics—spiritual laws also influence your daily professional life and carry a degree of cause and effect. Complying with them will bring benefits, and ignoring them will certainly result in negative consequences.

In the case of human laws against crimes such as murder and armed robbery, nobody is found "not guilty" by alleging that they weren't familiar with the law. The same is true with the spiritual laws. Therefore, it's important to know the twenty-five biblical "laws of success" and thereby avoid losing opportunities and money.

Some spiritual laws are so important that compliance is mandatory for those who desire to succeed in their careers. Failure to abide by these spiritual laws results in losses and defeats. Some spiritual laws work by expanding or maintaining success, while some are steps in a progression toward success.

Spiritual laws, such as those of wisdom, work, and sowing, among others, cannot be put on the back burner. Either you follow them or you won't get very far in your career—or in life. Other laws will serve to bring you greater personal equilibrium and happiness—for example, spiritual laws about serving your neighbor—but they aren't mandatory. One can be professionally and financially successful without becoming a philanthropist. Andrew Carnegie, Warren Buffett, and Bill Gates, however, decided to share their fortunes. It's a personal decision.

Abiding by the most important spiritual laws, or following all of them, and reaping the results is a personal decision. It's your choice.

If it is correct to say that the happiness of an achievement is impossible without the effort of striving for it, then it is also true that the more you apply the spiritual laws of success, the more successful you will be.

What Kind of Success Do You Desire?

Although this book is focused on professional success, it is good to remember there are other kinds of success—such as personal, spiritual, social, and financial—that you have to take under consideration in order to achieve a balance in your life.

A career and a paycheck are helpful, but they are not enough to make you happy and fulfilled. There will be moments when every one of us will face the questions: *Am I fulfilled? Do I enjoy what I do? Do I appreciate life?* These have nothing to do with money, market placement, or owning our own business. They are also unrelated to our assets. Living in a nice house and owning a great car are pleasant, for sure, but there are many people who own these things and are not satisfied.

Being interested only in professional and financial success and forgetting family and personal success, reputation, credibility, and social respect is a risk. Once more, this is an individual choice. Nevertheless, social respect, credibility, and a good reputation are strong aids to developing your career and increasing your finances. And, of course, health and family are indispensable to a better life.

There is another dimension of personal fulfillment beyond material success, which is characterized by an inner state of peace, security, gratitude, and happiness. As the Brazilian psychiatrist Roberto Shinyashiki has titled his bestseller, *Success Is Living Happily.*[1] To that end, we do not want you to be frustrated or miserable at work, restrained in your gifts, indebted, broken, or lacking in perspective.

We don't want this for ourselves or for our neighbors. This is why we will teach you the spiritual principles to follow to help you find a balance in your finances, your work, and your personal life, for happiness can be found only in the harmony of all three.

I had no ambition to make a fortune. Mere money-making has never been my goal; I had an ambition to build.
JOHN D. ROCKEFELLER

PART 1

Laws concerning Wisdom

1

The Law of Opportunity

> Your Father in heaven . . . causes his sun to rise on the
> evil and the good, and sends rain on the righteous and
> the unrighteous.
>
> MATTHEW 5:44–45

The Law of Opportunity says that everyone, at some point in his or her lifetime, will have an opportunity to get ahead in life. This means that even though we are affected by our social and economic background, access to education, culture, and family development, we can all rewrite our stories. If we are satisfied with our lives, then there is no need to change; but if we aren't, while we are alive we will have the opportunity to change course.

This spiritual law does not promise that all the opportunities will be the same but that everyone will have a fair share of them. We cannot assume that everyone will have the same sorts of opportunities. Unfortunately, it is not as simple as choosing to be rich and successful. These accomplishments depend on a number of circumstances, some that are the result of our personal choices and others that are outside of our control. However, no matter what, there is always something we can do to move forward toward success.

Happiness, as many say, is not a matter of circumstances but of how you deal with the circumstances you are given. In life you will be called to react to a number of things—some are foreseeable while others are unpredictable. The best you can do is learn how to seize the opportunities. Hence, your success doesn't depend on the number of chances you get but on the ones you take.

It is useless to compare yourself with others in terms of how lucky or unfortunate you are. That won't change a thing. We all have to play the hand we are dealt in life. You must move from where you are to where you want to be. For that, you have to be willing to pay the price and expend the time and the effort necessary to get there.

King Solomon is widely regarded as the wisest man who ever lived. The Bible says that God granted Solomon "a wise and discerning heart, so that there will never have been anyone like you, nor will there ever be" (1 Kings 3:12). In Solomon's biblical book of Ecclesiastes, he writes, "All share a common destiny—the righteous and the wicked, the good and the bad, the clean and the unclean, those who offer sacrifices and those who do not. As it is with the good, so with the sinful; as it is with those who take oaths, so with those who are afraid to take them" (9:2).

Exciting and mysterious but always surprising things happen to everyone in life. The strongest doesn't always win, and the cleverest doesn't always become rich. Again, Solomon says, "The race is not to the swift or the battle to the strong, nor does food come to the wise or wealth to the brilliant or favor to the learned; but time and chance happen to them all" (Eccles. 9:11).

We can observe that Solomon's statement is true: time and opportunity come to all. Whoever wins the race wins the medal. To the victor go the spoils. Therefore, success will come to those who, when their own time and chance happen, make the most of their opportunities.

Jesus also spoke of the Law of Opportunity. He illustrated this spiritual law through the following story:

> Therefore everyone who hears these words of mine and puts them into practice is like a wise man who built his house on the rock. The rain came down, the streams rose, and the winds blew and beat against that house; yet it did not fall, because it had its foundation on the rock. But everyone who hears these words of mine and does not put them into practice is like a foolish man who built his house on sand. The rain came down, the streams rose, and the winds blew and beat against that house, and it fell with a great crash. (Matt. 7:24–27)

The rain, the floods, and the winds affect everyone, but some have sound foundations and structures and others do not. Some roll their sleeves up and drill in stone, while others prefer the ease of building on sand. This is a product of the Law of Sowing, which says that we reap what we sow, as we are going to see later. Some lay solid foundations and they remain secure. Yet the Law of Opportunity was also in effect, since all had the chance to build and the rain fell on all of them.

These teachings of Solomon and Jesus warn us that bad weather, crises, calamities, opportunities, and changes in scenario affect everyone. Some will have the emotional, intellectual, financial, and relational foundations to weather the storms; others will not. The sun rises and the rain falls on everyone. Some are prepared for it and others are not. What about you? Are you ready to deal with the surprises life throws at you?

In our home country of Brazil, there is a saying: "The sun rises for everyone; the shade doesn't." This interesting concept implies that only those who have learned to deal with the sun are able to enjoy the shade. Only those who have built four walls and a roof over their heads are deserving of the shade. Even if you are hiding under a tree, you have to earn your shade by first moving under it.

At the beginning of the twentieth century, Andrew Carnegie hired Napoleon Hill to study the common ground of successful people. Hill spent over twenty years researching the lives of the most successful men of his time. He studied over sixteen thousand rich and powerful people in order to discover what they had in common. Among those he studied were the five hundred most important millionaires at that time, including Thomas Edison, Alexander Graham Bell, Henry Ford, Elmer Gates, Theodore Roosevelt, George Eastman, Woodrow Wilson, and John D. Rockefeller.

The results of Hill's research were summarized in 1937 in a book titled *Think and Grow Rich*. The book was submitted to the analysis of bankers, businesspersons, and university professors in order to correct or eliminate information lacking practical, scientific, or economic basis. Not a single modification was proposed.

Considered a treatise on the development of leadership, this book summarizes the laws that successful people follow, consciously or subconsciously. In the first chapter, Hill tells the story of Dr. Gunsaulus, a young pastor who announced to Chicago's newspapers that he would preach a sermon that Sunday called "What I Would Do If I Had a Million Dollars." Curious as to what he would hear, the meat-packing mogul Philip D. Armour decided to attend. In the sermon, the pastor laid out the well-structured plan for a technical college in which young people would develop the ability to think in a practical manner. The bottom line of the story is overwhelming.

After the sermon was over Mr. Armour walked down the aisle to the pulpit, introduced himself, and said: "Reverend, I liked your sermon. I believe you could do everything you said you would, if you had a million dollars. To prove that I believe in you and your sermon, if you will come to my office tomorrow morning, I will give you the million dollars."[1]

There is always plenty of capital for those who can create practical plans for using it.

You may not like the work in which you are now engaged. There are two ways of getting out of that work. One way is to take little interest in what you are doing, aiming merely to do enough to get by. Very soon you will find a way out, because the demand for your services will cease.

The other and better way is by making yourself so useful and efficient in what you are now doing that you will attract the favorable attention of those who have the power to promote you into more responsible work that is more to your liking. You may be surprised to discover that you are standing right over a rich mine.

To make a long story short, the sun rises for everyone, opportunities come along, but not everyone takes advantage of them.

Those who seize opportunities are more likely to fulfill their dreams.

Two men look out the same prison bars:
one sees mud and the other stars.
FREDERICK LANGBRIDGE

2

The Law of Wisdom

> Blessed are those who find wisdom, those who gain
> understanding, for she is more profitable than silver
> and yields better returns than gold. She is more pre-
> cious than rubies; nothing you desire can compare
> with her.
>
> PROVERBS 3:13–15

Wisdom is the foundation on which success is achieved. Some call
it organizational, strategic, or financial intelligence when choosing
what you want and how to get there. But when we follow the Law
of Wisdom, we can choose which seeds to sow and establish the
right causes in order to enjoy the desired results.

We are not talking about intelligence as in the ability to deal with
geometrical abstractions, mathematical calculations, or memory
tests but as the capacity to adapt while searching for happiness.
The intelligence we are talking about is synonymous with wisdom,

which is to know what, when, and how to do something and why it is worth doing. There are people who are very intelligent—with a high IQ and a prodigious capacity for reasoning and memory—but who lack wisdom for living. In this context, we are talking about not only so-called emotional intelligence but also a whole set of knowledge and abilities.

This greater intelligence, synonymous with wisdom, is the result of a combination of factors. One doesn't have to be born a genius; the means to happiness and success are readily available to us all, depending on our choices. You can become wise—all it takes is the desire to do so and a willingness to pay the price of obtaining knowledge and practicing intelligence.

Proverbs 3:13–15 reminds us that the best investment is not in gold or silver but in wisdom. After all, as another passage in Proverbs tells us, "By wisdom a house is built, and through understanding it is established; through knowledge its rooms are filled with rare and beautiful treasures. The wise prevail through great power, and those who have knowledge muster their strength. Surely you need guidance to wage war, and victory is won through many advisers" (24:3–6).

Wisdom should be a constant in everyone's life and involves three degrees or levels:

1. The first degree of wisdom is having wisdom in general, the necessary knowledge, good sense, and information to make the right choices and have the right attitudes in life.
2. The second degree of wisdom is a professional competence relating specifically to knowledge of how to work, which requires intelligence (in the sense of adaptation) and skill.

3. The third degree of wisdom involves in-depth knowledge, at the intimate level, of the necessary areas and people required for success.

The way to acquire these three levels of wisdom is to develop the ability to seek learning. You must be willing and humble enough to be open to learning, which will involve studying, reading the Bible and other books, examining your own experiences, and heeding the advice of a mentor, coach, teacher, friend, or coworker.

Today's job market is highly competitive; it is almost a daily battle to succeed. The Bible recommends that we be prudent in this battle and that we look for advisers to help us along the way. That is why it is wise to be always studying, so that our advisers (who may be authors of books we read, teachers, or coworkers) can help us conduct this war properly.

Which advisers have you been following? What was the last course you took, the last book you read, the last lecture you attended? When was the last time you asked a wise person for advice or turned to a professional coach or mentor?

The First Degree of Wisdom: Knowing What Values to Abide By

> Who is wise and understanding among you? Let them show it by their good life, by deeds done in the humility that comes from wisdom. (James 3:13)

This first and most important degree is wisdom in general. On a philosophical level, this kind of wisdom involves knowing what you want and where to go, making decisions, and searching for happiness and balance. It has a lot to do with the values you choose to guide your daily life and the guidelines by which you act and make decisions.

Values are like the guardrails on a freeway that help to keep you on the road. If you have ever driven on a dark, rainy night, you know what we are talking about. How many serious car accidents have been averted because of guardrails? By abiding by ethical standards, you are adopting guidelines that will help to keep you on the road to success.

There are many people who believe that maintaining ethical values will strip them of opportunities and the ability to compete in the market, but the example of the guardrail is a perfect proof of the contrary. Imagine a race with drivers going as fast as possible around a track. If a driver has a mishap, there is a safe zone where his car can stop—the guardrail. When it comes to business, those who leave the track come to a halt at the guardrails of morality, image, and credibility—and sometimes the guardrail of the law, which could cause them to lose time or even the possibility of staying in the race.

Shortcuts are not always the best way to get somewhere fast, and total freedom is not always positive. When you respect rules and limits, from those of etiquette to the law, you will gain a competitive edge in the long run.

The twenty-five biblical laws of success operate as bearing points to help you make decisions, to help you choose whether to go left or right, and to help you know when and how to turn the wheel correctly as you approach a curve in the road.

Each of us creates our own value system by adding personal experiences to what we learn from parents, school, church, friends, people we admire, and so on. The social and cultural arena to which we belong also exercises enormous influence on our values. Even television, movies, and online shows slowly, gradually, and in a constant and imperceptible manner, contribute to our beliefs and values.

Our attitudes, thoughts, and behaviors are the results of our values. They influence our choices, and as a logical next step, they define not only our results but also how far ahead we are capable of seeing. We can choose to abide by whichever values we embrace and to obey whichever rules we like. But these decisions and the resulting behaviors will determine our fate.

The Second Degree of Wisdom: Knowing How to Work

But go and learn. (Matt. 9:13)

Wisdom and competence are two different things. A competent person is not necessarily wise (and vice versa). People sometimes get confused because they define *wisdom* as knowing *how* to do something. But wisdom is knowing *what* to do. While competence resides on a practical level, wisdom works on a philosophical one. Wisdom and competence are closely related, but they are not the same thing. For example, a doctor can be extremely competent to perform surgery on a patient but not have the wisdom to deal with the patient or his family.

Thus when we talk of competence within the Law of Wisdom we mean to go one degree further. Knowing what to do is wisdom, but wisdom also includes knowing how to perform well on a job, how to be good at what you do.

Competence, therefore, demands intelligence and skill, which results in a very specific knowledge of how to get the job done, providing good service or a quality product.

Knowing How to Work Intelligently

Getting the job done is great, but you also need to be efficient, do the job well, and deliver excellent results. No one will put up with work badly done, only partially done, or done with no regard for technical standards. Nor is it wise to do fruitless work, something that has no outcome.

Sometimes we can do our job in a fruitless way. For example, consider someone who, instead of using a handcart, opts to carry bricks by hand. Our goal should be finishing a useful task in the most efficient and productive manner possible.

There are several examples of poor professionals, like the incompetent worker who doesn't know how to do his job and the lazy person who knows how to do the job but doesn't put in the effort. A common mistake is to rush through a task, leaving your job to a supervisor or a coworker who will have to fix or redo your work.

It's the combination of intelligence and willingness to work that makes someone a very desirable professional. This is a great competitive advantage.

Knowing How to Work Skillfully

There is a degree of skill that some people develop that makes them the best at what they do. In Brazil, we have a number of expressions to convey this idea, such as expertise, *savoir faire*, good will, or know-how.

The time when just having the energy and rolling up our sleeves were enough is long gone. We are now in the age of productivity, quality, and effectiveness. We need results. What's the use in giving someone a cake recipe if that person is like a fish out of water in the kitchen? You need someone with baking skills to get that job done.

What does the Bible say about being a skilled worker? Let's take a look at a few renderings of Proverbs 22:29 (emphasis added):

Do you see *someone skilled* in their work? They will serve before kings; they will not serve before officials of low rank.

Do you see people who work *skillfully*? They will work for kings but not work for lowly people. (CEB)

Skilled workers will always serve kings. They will never have to work for less important people. (ERV)

Show me *someone who does a good job* and I will show you someone who is better than most and worthy of the company of kings. (GNT)

Someone who works well and is skillful, clever, and dedicated will quickly reach the top. They will work for kings—in other words, for the best and for those who pay the best. A skillful, clever, and dedicated student will score the best grades, get the best scholarships, and get the most attractive job offers.

Whether you are a salesperson, carpenter, teacher, or business executive, devote yourself to what you do, develop the necessary skills, and you will find yourself among kings, moving up in life. That's the rule! It's quite simple really: be very good at what you do!

How can you be skilled and dedicated at work? By acquiring wisdom! Do you ask others how to do the job, or do people usually ask you how to do something? The first one to be promoted is usually the one who knows how to answer questions about what to do, how, when, where, and why.

If you know how to do your job well, sooner or later the spotlight will be on you. If not, then nothing will happen. You will end up either running circles in the same place or running the risk of going downhill.

A good example of how much a competent person is held in high esteem can be found in 1 Kings 7:13–14, a biblical passage that describes the precautions Solomon took while building his house:

> King Solomon sent to Tyre and brought Huram, whose mother was a widow from the tribe of Naphtali and whose father was from Tyre and a skilled craftsman in bronze. Huram was filled with wisdom, with understanding and with knowledge to do all kinds of bronze work. He came to King Solomon and did all the work assigned to him.

When you are competent and know what you're doing, people will notice, and employers will come after you.

> The one who gets wisdom loves life; the one who cherishes understanding will soon prosper. (Prov. 19:8)

The Third Degree of Wisdom: In-Depth Knowledge

> Be sure you know the condition of your flocks, give careful attention to your herds. (Prov. 27:23)

When talking about knowing the "condition of your flocks," the Bible is referring to how much you know about someone or something else, a degree of knowledge.

John Haggai, a Christian statesman and author of *Lead On! Leadership That Endures in a Changing World*, tells in his lectures the story of an American businessman who wanted to expand his business to Indonesia. When he arrived at the airport he rented space at the business center, called a local executive, and left a message stating: "Come to the airport. I've rented the VIP room. Bring your wife, and let's talk business! We have until 5:30 p.m., when my flight leaves for Sydney."

By failing to do research—that is, for lack of in-depth knowledge of the cultural norms—this businessman missed an opportunity by committing at least four mistakes:

1. Local protocol in Indonesia is to go to the person, not have them come to you.

2. According to local practice, you should never invite family members to business meetings.

3. It's not considered polite to talk business at the first meeting.

4. Saying what time you have to leave is considered offensive; it sends the message that "my schedule is more important than yours."

This was a case of cultural insensitivity, but it's a good example of how not knowing your subject or client can lead to unnecessary losses.

Do you know who and what are the "sheep" that interest you? Who are the people or things about which you need in-depth information? Do you know the people you're dealing with? Do you have in-depth knowledge of the business they work for or the company at which you want to be hired? Do you have an intimate level of knowledge about the business you want to start?

Your "sheep" may be the people under your command or to whom you report. Your "sheep" may be the company where you work, whether a family business or a multinational corporation. The fact that the company doesn't belong to you is no excuse for not getting to know it. And if you do own your own company, that is all the more reason to be aware of all that is going on around you. If you know who plays the role of the "sheep" in your professional life, and if you dedicate yourself to knowing their condition well, then you will be on the right path to success.

There are people who sell sandwiches on the beach but cannot do the math properly, so they end up working for nothing. If they add up the cost of all the ingredients, the bus fare to and from the beach, and their other expenses, they will discover that they are not making any profit. And this can happen to large companies as well. If the publisher of this book does not correctly calculate the cost of the paper, printing, design, proofreading, distribution, fixed costs, and so on, they may face a loss. If each book sells for twenty dollars but costs twenty-one dollars to publish, the greater the sales, the deeper the losses.

There are those who don't know how much they owe the bank and others who do not keep a record of their debts because they are afraid of knowing the actual amount. This intentional ignorance doesn't help; rather, it gets in the way of success. When you are buying a car, it is important to know not only the monthly payments but also the interest and depreciation, or you will end up paying the equivalent of three cars. How can anyone prosper like that?

To summarize, the recommendation of the Bible is "go and learn" (Matt. 9:13). We find this principle again in the advice given in Genesis: "Rule over" (1:28).

Find out what you have to do and how to do it. Know the people you have to deal with: coworkers, bosses, clients. Find out everything there is to know about the company for which you work—its requirements, products, and needs. And know it well, deeply and intimately.

If you need more incentive to learn well the condition of your flock, check the warning in this verse: "For riches do not endure forever, and a crown is not secure for all generations" (Prov. 27:24).

It's important to know the real situation of your company and your market and to commit wholeheartedly to your business and your career. Knowing the condition of the company is also useful in letting you know when it is time to make a change, to innovate, or even to shut down and start anew.

> *Gold there is, and rubies in abundance, but lips*
> *that speak knowledge are a rare jewel.*
> PROVERBS 20:15

3

The Law of Vision

Then the LORD replied: "Write down the revelation
and make it plain on tablets so that a herald may run
with it."

HABAKKUK 2:2

Strategic planning in any company begins with the company's vision. The vision is where the company sees itself in the future—where it wants to be and how it wants to be known.

The Law of Vision tells you that you need to be clear about what you want in life. What is your vision? What do you live for? Where do you want to go? How do you want to be known? It's your choice. You might change your mind later, but you must define these concepts to be able to move forward.

Perhaps you have already dealt with strategic planning on your day-to-day job, but what about your life? Have you analyzed what your personal vision is? Have you studied your strengths and weaknesses? What about the opportunities and threats ahead of you?

Some like to call their personal vision a dream. You can call it what you like: vision, dream, goal, objective, or purpose. The important thing is to know what you are looking for. Without purpose there will be no progress. You need to have wishes, dreams, and plans. If you want your vision to come true, you need to lay this foundation for success.

Once we establish our vision, we are able to set our priorities in order to direct our efforts. There are a number of different kinds of success—personal, spiritual, social, family, and financial success. Each one has its place and importance. That is why achieving a reasonable and balanced success in each area accounts for our idea of prosperity.

Yes, you can enjoy success in several different areas. It might not be easy, but it is definitely possible. However, you need to know where you are going before you start walking.

Solomon, the wisest man who ever lived, said, "Better a small serving of vegetables with love than a fattened calf with hatred" (Prov. 15:17). This statement reveals that money, although it has its uses, is not the sole measure of success. If we invest too much in financial success and forget family success, we are making a dangerous choice.

So take a moment to think about the following questions:

What defines success for you?

How do you approach success? (Is it a good thing? Is it your priority?)

How do you think you can achieve success?

What means have you been using or do you intend to use in order to achieve success?

How well do you handle money?

When considering your vision, it is worthwhile having answers to these questions. Regardless of your concept of success, however, there is one thing that is certain: success will not be achieved without a considerable degree of effort and a willingness to take risks.

Fortunately, *success* and *failure* are not labels to use on people but only on situations. Success and failure are two sides of the same coin, a picture of the results of a certain moment, consequences of a given set of choices and circumstances from the past. New mental and behavioral choices can change your reality. It's all a matter of cause and effect or, in Jesus's words, sowing and reaping, as we will discuss later.

Imagination

> We are such stuff as dreams are made on.
>
> William Shakespeare

The basic requirement, the special ingredient, for developing your vision is imagination. Solomon says, "For as he thinks within himself, so he is" (Prov. 23:7 ISV).

You have to figure out your own vision. For that you will need a bit of dreaming, a tad of courage, and a pinch of boldness. The idea is to think outside the box. The box might be shyness, fear, or any other limitation set by yourself or others in the pursuit of your dreams. Imagination can build anything. Imagine big accomplishments, and you will be big; imagine small steps, and you will be small. Therefore, think big.

> *Obstacles are those frightful things you see*
> *when you take your eyes off your goal.*
> HENRY FORD

4

The Law of Focus

I do not run like someone running aimlessly; I do not
fight like a boxer beating the air.

1 CORINTHIANS 9:26

Your vision is a snapshot of the future, but to get there you need
to stay focused. That's why you need to know the Law of Focus.

What you focus on, what you pay attention to, expands as you
move closer to your vision. Jesus said that where someone deposits
what is most important to them, that is where their heart will be.
And of course, your heart is the field in which you will advance:
"For where your treasure is, there your heart will be also" (Luke
12:34).

Seneca, one of the greatest thinkers of the Roman Empire, reportedly observed, "If one does not know to which port one is
sailing, no wind is favorable." It is up to you to focus on a goal—
preferably in a field in which, out of vocation or preparation, you

have a good chance of making a name for yourself. We all have abilities and characteristics that help us become more successful in some situations than others.

Instead of thinking about the gap that currently separates you from your goals, focus on a shift in performance. If you follow the biblical laws of success that you are learning in this book, you will be closer to achieving what you desire. Remember that time goes by regardless. Make sure you develop along with it. In a world that doesn't stop, where change is the only constant, if you stand still you will be left behind. So you have to keep moving.

One of the ways to develop your focus is to establish daily, weekly, monthly, and yearly plans. Set them in your mind and then write them down on paper (or on your computer, tablet, or phone). Write out where you want to be next year, in five years, and in ten or twenty years. Studies show that written goals are easier to achieve than those we keep only in our minds.

One suggestion is to make a daily to-do list, even for minor things. When you complete a task, place a check mark beside it or draw a line through it. This gives you a feeling of "mission accomplished." When things on your list don't get done or when you are unable to complete a task, review and revise your plans. Decide whether a particular task is achievable. Checklists are great for everything from groceries to school supplies to what to pack in your suitcase before a trip.

Don't get disheartened if you can't do everything on your list. And keep the lists, because in one, five, or ten years you will see that those things on which you focused were achieved, whereas others to which you put less effort (but that may have been equally important) were not.

If the size of the task frightens you, if you slack off, if you don't follow through, believe me, in five or ten years you will be the same or worse off than today. The things that depend on you must be done in the best possible way so as to ensure the continuity of your success. So get moving!

In his lectures, Rubens usually gives the following advice: "Focus on a target within a given period. Five years is a good cycle. If in five years you follow the principles of success, this time frame will enable you to measure just how far you have come. If you waste time on useless things, you will certainly pay the price."

Establish your personal goals and a time frame in which to accomplish them. This is where your success will start.

Focus versus Sacrifice

> The kingdom of heaven is like a merchant looking for fine pearls. When he found one of great value, he went away and sold everything he had and bought it. (Matt. 13:45–46)

To focus means to sacrifice. The tale of the merchant tells of a man who found something so perfect that he sacrificed what he had in order to realize his dream. This section considers the relationship between focus and sacrifice. No one can focus on anything if at the same time they don't have the courage to sacrifice something else.

Jesus said, "Unless a kernel of wheat falls to the ground and dies, it remains only a single seed. But if it dies, it produces many seeds" (John 12:24). This tells us that every job, every achievement, requires from us some kind of sacrifice. Just as important as knowing what you want and focusing on your vision is knowing what you have to sacrifice and then making that sacrifice.

Success always demands some sacrifice, so does failure. Notice how both success and failure come at a price. The price of success usually comes first, and the person enjoys life afterward. Failure usually happens to those who don't make an effort at the outset. They pay the price later.

The Bible says that there is food that tastes sweet to begin with, but bitter later. "So I went to the angel and asked him to give me the little scroll. He said to me, 'Take it and eat it. It will turn your stomach sour, but "in your mouth it will be as sweet as honey"'" (Rev. 10:9). Professional life is very similar. Not making the proper sacrifices now may appear sweet, but the aftertaste is a bitter one.

Focus versus Positive Thinking

Set your minds on things above, not on earthly things. (Col. 3:2)

Our brains are programmed by our thoughts. The more you think about good and positive things, the more good and positive things will happen. Surely our thoughts alone don't change reality—some action is due, as well as a dose of sacrifice and persistence. But everything starts in your mind. There are studies pointing out that people who think positively tend to get better results.[1]

When the Bible tells us to strive for the things above, it is also telling us to look for loftier goals, to strive for better ideas and thoughts.

41

Finally, brothers and sisters, whatever is true, whatever is noble, whatever is right, whatever is pure, whatever is lovely, whatever is admirable—if anything is excellent or praiseworthy—think about such things.

PHILIPPIANS 4:8

5

The Law of Planning

The plans of the diligent lead to profit.

PROVERBS 21:5

Anyone intending to be successful cannot ignore the Law of Planning. This biblical law is illustrated by the following words of Jesus:

Suppose one of you wants to build a tower. Won't you first sit down and estimate the cost to see if you have enough money to complete it? For if you lay the foundation and are not able to finish it, everyone who sees it will ridicule you, saying, "This person began to build and wasn't able to finish."

Or suppose a king is about to go to war against another king. Won't he first sit down and consider whether he is able with ten thousand men to oppose the one coming against him with twenty thousand? If he is not able, he will send a delegation while the other is still a long way off and will ask for terms of peace. (Luke 14:28–32)

The planning stage of any task is paramount to the successful execution of the project. It is not our intent in this book to give you full instructions about planning, but we want you to be aware that planning is an essential step. In order to achieve lasting success, you need to incorporate this concept and seek out books and courses that teach you how to organize and plan your life and your career.[1]

There are three levels of planning:

1. Overall, strategic, long-term planning
2. Planning for shorter periods (every other week, a month, trimester, a year)
3. Weekly and daily planning

Many people believe that making plans is boring or difficult, so they never learn how to plan. The problem is that planning avoids suffering and waste.

People with surplus resources don't have to worry as much about planning. But that is not reality for the majority of people. Imagine you are trying to buy a house. If you do your research first, you will choose the best option, taking into account the condition of the property, the price, and the payment terms. If you don't do the research, you will likely fail to get the best deal because you didn't plan ahead.

Professionals who plan well will stand out in the market. Many cultures do not leave space for planning, especially long-term planning. In Brazil, for example, we live in a culture of instant rewards and where things end up being done at the last minute. This was made clear in the lack of planning for the infrastructure required for major events such as the World Cup and the

Olympics. If you plan ahead, then you are already better than average.

The first step in planning is deciding what you want. Whether your plan is for achieving the final or an intermediate objective, whether your plan includes stages or not, establish beforehand a plan for what you intend to do.

SWOT Analysis

> May he give you the desire of your heart and make all your plans succeed. (Ps. 20:4)

There are a variety of systems and tools available to teach you how to plan effectively, and, as we mentioned previously, there are many helpful courses and books on the subject. One widely used corporate management tool is the SWOT Analysis, which provides a picture of a company's internal and external environments. This technique is credited to Albert Humphrey who did research at Stanford University in the 1960s and '70s based on data about the Fortune 500—the five hundred largest corporations ranked by *Fortune* magazine. This analysis will help you define the strategic actions you will need to adopt as you identify the positive and negative factors you will have to face.

SWOT is an acronym for Strengths, Weaknesses, Opportunities, and Threats. The purpose of the SWOT Analysis system is to analyze the internal environment's strengths and weaknesses and the external environment's opportunities and threats. This analysis looks at qualities and deficiencies on the internal level and analyzes ease and difficulty on the external level. It can easily be applied to both professional and personal levels.

To know if this tool can help you, ask yourself the following questions:

Strengths

What are you (your company, product, team) good at?

What special resources do you possess or have on hand?

What differentiates you from others? How and where can you enhance these advantages?

What do other people think you are good at?

In what type of activity do you excel?

Weaknesses

What are your flaws?

What do you need to improve?

Where are you less capable or qualified than the average person or the people with whom you coexist?

What can you change in order to improve?

Which of your qualities offset your weaknesses?

Can you hire someone or employ some tool to offset your weaknesses?

What things (flaws, weaknesses, habits, problems) do others complain about in you?

Opportunities

What external opportunities have you identified?

What can you do for yourself, for the company, and for customers that could be used as an opportunity?

What external circumstances may help you?

What allies and resources are available to you but which you are currently not using (for example, scholarships, books, courses, experienced friends)?

Which allies and resources are not available to you but might be if you made an effort?

Threats

What external difficulties are thwarting your plans?

Which events or circumstances may adversely affect you?

Which external problems can you resolve or minimize?

What strategies can you adopt to overcome these difficulties?

After answering these questions it will be easier to create a strategic action plan for you or your product, service, or company.

Jesus gave a good illustration of the importance of planning so as not to miss opportunities in his parable of the ten young maidens waiting for the groom's arrival:

> Five of them were foolish and five were wise. The foolish ones took their lamps but did not take any oil with them. The wise ones, however, took oil in jars along with their lamps. The bridegroom was a long time in coming, and they all became drowsy and fell asleep.
>
> At midnight the cry rang out: "Here's the bridegroom! Come out to meet him!"
>
> Then all the virgins woke up and trimmed their lamps. The foolish ones said to the wise, "Give us some of your oil; our lamps are going out."
>
> "No," they replied, "there may not be enough for both us and you. Instead, go to those who sell oil and buy some for yourselves."

But while they were on their way to buy the oil, the bridegroom arrived. The virgins who were ready went in with him to the wedding banquet. And the door was shut.

Later the others also came. "Lord, Lord," they said, "open the door for us!"

But he replied, "Truly I tell you, I don't know you." (Matt. 25:2–12)

Opportunity doesn't always arrive when we would prefer it to, but when it does, it should not find us wanting. Proper planning and preparation are the solution.

Another name for this prior action is prudence. *Prudence* can be defined in the following ways: "1. Careful or wise in handling practical matters; exercising good judgment or common sense: *a prudent manager of money.* 2. Characterized by or resulting from care or wisdom in practical matters or in planning for the future: *a prudent investment.*"[2]

And what does Jesus tell us to do? "Be ye therefore prudent as serpents and innocent as doves" (Matt. 10:16 JUB).

Unplanned actions are a display not of courage but of foolishness. In this sense Solomon says, "The wise fear the LORD and shun evil, but a fool is hotheaded and yet feels secure" (Prov. 14:16). In this same vein William Shakespeare said, "A fool's bolt is soon shot."[3] Haste and the failure to plan are all counterproductive.

The Importance of Time Management

Make the most of every opportunity. (Col. 4:5)

Planning is not something that you can do once and never do again. It is an everyday labor. Just as we need to plan for the future (one, five, ten years ahead), we need to plan our days, our weeks, and our months. As Scripture points out: "Be very careful, then, how you live—not as unwise but as wise, making the most of every opportunity" (Eph. 5:15–17).

Excelling in time management is vital to success. The better you are at managing your time, the better your days will be. We all have twenty-four hours a day. We all have the same amount of time to work on our dreams and our career. Some people may have a better financial or intellectual situation, which brings them some advantages, but if this is not your case, do not be jealous. We each have personal challenges we must face.

Learn how to manage your time and to be present and focused in each and every one of your activities. It is also important for you to set time aside to rest and reenergize after a long day. We will discuss this in greater detail when talking about the Law of Recharging.

Solomon talks about this in the book of Ecclesiastes:

> There is a time for everything,
>   and a season for every activity under the heavens:
>
>   a time to be born and a time to die,
>   a time to plant and a time to uproot,
>   a time to kill and a time to heal,
>   a time to tear down and a time to build,
>   a time to weep and a time to laugh,
>   a time to mourn and a time to dance,
>   a time to scatter stones and a time to gather them,
>   a time to embrace and a time to refrain from
>   embracing,
>   a time to search and a time to give up,

a time to keep and a time to throw away,
a time to tear and a time to mend,
a time to be silent and a time to speak,
a time to love and a time to hate,
a time for war and a time for peace.

What do workers gain from their toil? I have seen the burden God has laid on the human race. He has made everything beautiful in its time. He has also set eternity in the human heart; yet no one can fathom what God has done from beginning to end. I know that there is nothing better for people than to be happy and to do good while they live. That each of them may eat and drink, and find satisfaction in all their toil—this is the gift of God. (3:1–13)

We suggest that you learn more about time management. There are multiple books available through which you can learn techniques and tips to manage your calendar.[4] Keeping a timetable is one of the many options available. Despite being a great tool, many look on it with suspicion, believing they will become slaves to the timetable. That's nonsense. A timetable, calendar, or planner is designed to help you plan all your activities, leaving space for family, study, work, and health and giving you freedom, flexibility, and efficiency. With proper planning you will enjoy a better life and be better equipped for the future.

It's important to continue practicing time management even after building a career or company. Success may bring all sorts of opportunities your way—good and bad (invitations, proposals, personal attacks, and so on)—and you must be prepared for them. One piece of advice is to learn how to say no. Learn how to say no to resentment as well as to an invitation that doesn't fit your timetable.

If you don't learn how to say no, you are setting yourself up for failure, because you may not have time to plan and learn and maintain your professional success. Ultimately, you could lose track of family, friends, and all the things you cherish the most.

He who fails to plan is planning to fail.
WINSTON CHURCHILL

PART 2

Laws concerning Work

6

The Law of Work

All hard work brings a profit, but mere talk leads only
to poverty.

PROVERBS 14:23

Do you know the riddle of the three frogs on a leaf? Well, there
are three frogs on a leaf and one of them decides to jump into the
water. How many frogs are left on the leaf?

Think for a moment before giving an answer, because it's not
as obvious as it seems.

The correct answer is three frogs, because one of them decided
to jump—but the riddle doesn't say that he did jump. Quite often,
we behave like the frog in the story. We decide to do this or that,
but in the end we do nothing.

We have many decisions to make in life: some easy, some difficult. Most of the mistakes we make are not due to wrong decisions;

they are due to indecision, omissions, and inaction out of fear that something will go wrong.

Action does indeed involve risks, but we have to face those risks, because the biggest failure in life lies in doing nothing. The Law of Work says that people who don't take action don't accomplish anything, and their lives become meaningless. They may avoid experiencing pain, but they don't learn, they don't feel, they don't change, they don't grow, and they don't live. They are like slaves who fear freedom. Only those who take risks are free.

Action takes two principal forms: study and work. Studying is a form of work because it gives you knowledge and wisdom. As a rule, it takes a long period of study not only to attain know-how but also certain positions at work and a good salary. But even when you reach the top, you should never stop studying.

Since the world doesn't stand still and human knowledge grows on a daily basis, we must be continual learners. Therefore, studying is not only part of the process of finding a good job or growing a business, it should also be part of the daily routine of any professional who wants to keep his position in the market. But studying alone won't solve everything.

To say that the only place where success comes before work is in the dictionary is a cliché, but it's a fact. When properly understood, this realization can lead to professional success. If the connection between work and success is ignored, it causes misunderstanding and wastes time and money.

Work breeds success. And work begins with the search for knowledge, whether by studying or gaining practical experience.

One of the many traps on the way to success is taking shortcuts. Sometimes the best way is not the shortest or the easiest. The results can be very positive if success takes a long time to achieve. Early success can lead to a negative outcome, because wisdom and the ability to manage often come only with time.

The Law of Work is a powerful spiritual law because, as a rule, those who achieve success or money without honest, hard work are unable to hold on to either for very long. "Dishonest money dwindles away, but whoever gathers money little by little makes it grow" (Prov. 13:11).

Confidence

> Whether you think you can, or you think you can't—you're right.
>
> Henry Ford

For your work to bear fruit, one ingredient is indispensable: confidence. You must believe in yourself and in your vision. Believe in what your business is creating or managing.

The Bible says, "Whoever plows and threshes should be able to do so in the hope of sharing in the harvest" (1 Cor. 9:10). Nothing will happen unless you believe in it. Without faith nothing is possible because "faith is confidence in what we hope for and assurance about what we do not see" (Heb. 11:1). The Bible says that "through faith and patience" we "inherit what has been promised" (Heb. 6:12). We are not talking about religious faith, but faith in yourself and in what you do.

There are countless studies and surveys that show that believing in yourself and in your projects is necessary for achieving success, for being motivated, and for facing the inherent difficulties of any undertaking.[1] If you don't have faith in your project, company, or product, then nobody will. Therefore, have faith.

Dedication

Whatever your hand finds to do, do it with all your might. (Eccles. 9:10)

Working is not enough. You must devote yourself to it. There are many companies, employees, and service providers who do not follow this spiritual law, instead adopting the habit of doing as little as possible—and thereby reducing their growth prospects as well.

When you do your work with true devotion, rather than just to keep up appearances, recognition is sure to follow. It doesn't matter what label people may put on you (insane, workaholic, yes-man), stay focused and keep on working.

A company that behaves in this manner will be a market winner; a professor or lecturer who behaves like this will never be out of work. Dedication to your work is a concept with a religious bias that, when applied, delivers not only spiritual results (for those who believe) but also professional and secular ones.

The Bible is emphatic on this point: if you want a better life, learn to work well and to work hard, be competent and dedicated, and put your whole heart into it. "Whatever you do, work at it with all your heart" (Col. 3:23).

We can also liken dedication to enthusiasm. Napoleon Hill says that enthusiasm is the fuel that drives men and women toward great discoveries and achievements.[2] Achievers have a profound passion for their objectives. They not only show great personal enthusiasm but also arouse the same sentiment in those around them and in their team, regardless of the external conditions.

So if you want to be successful, learn to love what you are aiming for and sow enthusiasm in yourself and in those around you.

Learn to have a passion for life. Be aware that enthusiasm—and the lack of it—are contagious.

Dedication also involves persistence and effort. Solomon recommends, "Sow your seed in the morning and at evening let your hands not be idle, for you do not know which will succeed, whether this or that, or whether both will do equally well" (Eccles. 11:6).

Solomon also says, "When there are no oxen, the manger is empty, but from the strength of an ox come abundant harvests" (Prov. 14:4). What does he mean by this? First, Solomon is explaining that the harder you work, the greater your results will be. If you leave the production site empty, it appears to be fine. But productivity comes from filling the empty spaces. We have to fill our professional sphere with actions in order to obtain growth. Dealing with an ox is definitely laborious, but it also pays off.

Furthermore, Solomon is implying that if you use your tools properly your productivity will increase. If you own a farm and want an ox, you must know that the animal will give you a lot of work. You will have to look after it, feed and water it, and clean up after it. You'll have more to do on the farm. In exchange, the ox will help with your work at harvesttime and you will have a bigger harvest. In order to grow your earnings, you have to work in a smarter and more efficient manner. Your product will have added value.

There are professionals who prefer the comfort zone, which may be risk free but also results in a lack of maturity and success. What type of professional are you? The kind who turns down the ox so as not to have more work, but thereby turning your back on an abundant harvest? Or are you the type of professional with the courage to take on more work or to better yourself, in order to enjoy a more abundant harvest or a bigger paycheck? What sort of equipment, programs, and tools would make your life easier and more productive? Perhaps there are tools that you haven't given a thought to using.

What do you have in your professional "barn"? It may be clean (as well it should!), but only in the sense of being tidy and organized, never empty due to a lack of productivity.

Persistence

> If the ax is dull and its edge unsharpened, more strength is needed, but skill will bring success. (Eccles. 10:10)

Persistence is fundamental when it comes to working well, because it implies an attitude, a state of mind, and a willingness to win. Hannibal, the Carthaginian general who conquered Rome, reportedly told his subordinates, "I shall either find a way or make one." Or, as the Latin proverb says, "If there is no wind, row."

Ecclesiastes 10:10 is telling us that when your ax is blunt, you can either sharpen it or hit harder. One way or another, you will cut down the tree.

If your ax isn't working, if what you are doing is not getting results, then you have two choices: either you try harder or you get sharper. If you are failing a test or unable to make a sale, maybe you are striking too hard and exhausting yourself.

Sharpening the ax is cleverer than striking harder. This can be better understood from the tale of a strong lumberjack who wanted to break the record of seventy-two trees felled in a day. On the first try he managed to cut down seventy trees. The following day, he woke up a little earlier and worked really hard, but he cut down only sixty-eight trees. The next day, he got up even earlier and tried even harder, working himself to exhaustion, but cut down only sixty trees. Frustrated, he sat down to rest. An older and more experienced lumberjack felt sorry for the young man and, sitting down beside him, asked, "Son, how much time did you set aside for sharpening the ax?"

The more you use the ax, the more its edge dulls and becomes less effective, unless you sharpen it again. Learn to sharpen your ax. Even if you are at the top of your productivity score, there is always room for improvement. Don't settle for less. It is always possible to do a better job, which will lead to a better life and greater well-being for all.

If you have the choice, opt for sharpening your ax. If you lack proper conditions or the proper tools, the best scenario is to work harder, putting in more effort and energy.

Many people complain that they do their job well but get no recognition. Their bosses don't value them; others make fun of them or stand in their way professionally. That was what happened to Rubens, as we will see in his own words.

I had a tough life. My parents were great people, and they managed to raise six kids while making minimum wage. We were extremely poor. I studied in public schools up to my junior year in high school. In my senior year, my older brother became a sergeant and decided to pay for my last year of high school. In this high-level private school I was bullied constantly. People would call me names and I was discouraged from going on with my studies, under the idea that I would not be accepted to any university.

However, I did well in my acceptance exams and decided to go to a military academy, where I continued to face discouragement. I could not swim and almost drowned a few times but I refused to give up. After graduation, as an infantryman, I decided to apply to engineering school in a military institution, even facing harsh criticism. I was accepted.

After graduation, I was serving as a captain of the Brazilian army, based in the State of Acre, when I decided to become a public servant working as an analyst for the Federal Bank of Brazil (Central Bank). In Brazil, to join public service one must pass highly selective public examinations. While I was preparing for the exams, my pregnant wife suffered from preeclampsia. Even with my wife and child at risk, without the proper books or means, I passed the exams and joined the Central Bank.

As an analyst I had to deal with coworkers questioning my motives for studying so hard. In their eyes, I was already a public servant and I could not be let go, so what else was I looking for? Recognition? I got my PhD while working as an analyst, and most of the time I was criticized because my thesis was unrelated to my day-to-day work. I had to overcome all this, but it was worth it. My thesis received an award from the Brazilian government because of its importance in the field of public policy. It was published and recognized not only internally but abroad.

People did not have faith in me, but I had faith in myself and kept moving forward.

When someone tried to discredit me, I responded with hard work and attention to details, keeping mistakes to a minimum. I never ceased to help those around me, even the ones who didn't believe in my dreams. I knew that one day my time would come. I put my faith in God, but I had to overcome the obstacles of lack of credit, disrespect, humiliation, persecution, lack of prestige, and poverty.

That's the reason I believe that there is no victory for those who give up. Only the ones who persevere will succeed in life.

When the path is unknown, persistence is more important than intelligence.

Details of my life story—the hope, the faith, and the measures I took to overcome challenges—can be found in my biography.[3] In order to succeed, I would do it all over again.

Rubens lives by Colossians 3:23: "Whatever you do, work at it with all your heart," a piece of advice we should follow in our professional lives as much as in our personal ones.

There is a line that became popular in Brazil from the Brazilian movie *Elite Squad*, which portrays the Special Operations Unit of Rio de Janeiro's police: "If you can't handle it, bail out!"[4] The unit also has an interesting expression repeated over and over again to those who complain about the tough training: "You knew it was hell. You came because you wanted to."[5] Professional success is sort of like that: it is hard, and at times we may even want to bail out, but those who stay and fight are the ones who make their dreams come true.

Matthew 7:8 says, "For everyone who asks receives; the one who seeks finds; and to the one who knocks, the door will be opened." That's perseverance. If you can't sharpen the ax, then strike harder until the wood is cut.

The pessimist complains about the wind, the optimist hopes it changes, and the realist sets his sail.
WILLIAM ARTHUR WARD

7

The Law of Courage

If you falter in a time of trouble, how small is your strength!

PROVERBS 24:10

The Law of Courage speaks to the willingness to take risks. The Bible talks of a frightened servant who, for lack of courage, did not invest the money he received from his boss, and so he was fired (Matt. 25:14–30). In the story, Jesus says that a man needed to leave the country, so he "called his servants and entrusted his wealth to them" (v. 14). To one of them he gave five bags of gold (the cash equivalent of a year's salary); to another, two; and to another, one. He distributed the bags of gold according to the ability of each servant.

The servant who received five bags of gold went immediately to trade with them and earned another five. Likewise, the one who received two made another two. But the servant who received one bag "went off, dug a hole in the ground, and hid his master's money" (v. 18).

After some time the boss returned and called his servants to account. The first two had not been idle and didn't miss the opportunity to make more money, and they received their master's praise. The third servant, however, who had hid the money out of fear or insecurity, made no return. Of course the owner of the goods was not at all content. He confiscated the bag of gold, accused him of being lazy, and said, "You should have put my money on deposit with the bankers, so that when I returned I would have received it back with interest" (v. 27). The frightened servant had thrown away the opportunity to invest and make a return on the money entrusted to him.

All investments require strategic analysis and carry implicit risk. Many people fail to be bold with their investments, preferring to be prudent. We cannot be so bold as to be irresponsible, nor can we be excessively prudent to the point of being lazy, negligent, or content with our lot.

Niccolò Machiavelli, in his classic *The Prince*, says, "A prince being thus obliged to know well how to act as a beast must imitate the fox and the lion, for the lion cannot protect himself from snares, and the fox cannot defend himself from wolves. One must therefore be a fox to recognize snares, and a lion to frighten wolves."[1] Machiavelli counsels the prince to avail himself of his characteristics in such a manner as to be successful at a time when he would be required to be either more prudent or more daring.

There are times for being as daring as a lion and times for being as prudent as a fox.

We all know people who have no courage to move on and no determination to make a return on what they have, whether it is money or talent (skill). In the end they bury everything. What a waste!

Don't be concerned with how much money you have, but rather with how much of a return you can make on it in order to grow and prosper. However, if you exceed the limits or are reckless, daring will not justify your lack of caution. You must seek wisdom and moderation in order to manage your talents and finances well.

Initiative

Strong men retain riches. (Prov. 11:16 KJV)

Courage also means initiative. As a boy, David faced the giant Goliath. He seized the initiative: he got on with it and attacked first, instead of waiting to be attacked (1 Sam. 17:48). Those who take the initiative are at a huge advantage. Al Ries and Jack Trout teach this in *The 22 Immutable Laws of Marketing*: "It is better to be first than to be better."[2]

Bravery and daring bring riches, but kindness adds to them respect. "A kindhearted woman gains honor, but ruthless men gain only wealth" (Prov. 11:16). Both are possible. You can be bold in ideas and execution but kind and gentle in manner, even when you need to be firm. This idea is expressed in the Latin phrase *suaviter in modo, fortiter in re*—in other words, "gently in manner, strongly in deed."

Calculated Risk

> Whoever digs a pit may fall into it;
>> Whoever breaks through a wall may be bitten by a
>> snake.
> Whoever quarries stones may be injured by them;
>> whoever splits logs may be endangered by them.
>> (Eccles. 10:8–9)

In Ecclesiastes 10:8–9, Solomon points out that digging pits and breaking through walls are risky jobs. But there are some risks that, even with a high probability of problems, may be worth it. It has been said, "If you want to avoid irritation, don't own a business." In other words, owning a business is a guarantee of problems, but those problems might be worth having.

The Bible warns us that a person who carries stones may get hurt. However, if you want to build a sturdy house or a wall or a bridge, it's better to work with stone than with straw or sand.

A challenge requires work if it is to be overcome. If you own a business, you will have problems; if you are taking a test or attending college you will certainly have headaches. If you want to build something big, you'll have to carry more stones than if your goal is to make only something small. It's worth recalling the story of the "Three Little Pigs." The only pig who was safe from the big bad wolf was the one who had put in the most work to build a brick house.

Whoever chops wood is taking a risk, but he is the one who gets to make a fire. For example, read the following statement from William:

> When I first released my book, *Como Passar em Provas e Concursos* (*How to pass tests and public examinations*), I took a risk.[3] Nobody

wanted to publish it; no one thought it would sell. But I insisted and decided to publish it myself because I believed in my book.

I believed, and I asked God for his blessing. Then I took all the precautions, took out a loan, and published the book. Again, I wasn't acting impulsively, my risk had been calculated. This book has sold over two hundred thousand copies so far, covering the previous loan and granting other financial and professional benefits.

Depending on the situation it may be more dangerous not to take a risk than to take a calculated one. It has been said that you don't jump over a cliff with two jumps. Ralph Waldo Emerson stated, "In skating over thin ice, our safety is in our speed."[4] On the other hand, boldness without caution is madness. Taking a chance on something does not mean flying blindly into it. It is to assume risks with courage, wisdom, and planning. With proper care, risk can transform into opportunity. We should be like those who encouraged the biblical priest Ezra to take a risk, saying, "Take courage and do it" (Ezra 10:4).

Nick Vujicic—an Australian entrepreneur, preacher, and panelist born without his upper and lower limbs—makes a similar claim in his book *Life Without Limits*. He separates ridiculous risks (the ones you are prepared for) from stupid risks (the ones that are too crazy to even be considered). In his words:

You should never take a risk in which you could lose more than you could win. Ridiculous risk, however, is taking a chance that looks or sounds crazier than it really is because:

1. You've prepared yourself.
2. You have reduced the risk as much as possible.
3. You have a backup plan if things go wrong.[5]

If you roll up your sleeves and get to work, you will obtain stones and firewood. If you don't want to take risks for fear of getting hurt, then you will have nothing. Which do you prefer?

Life shrinks or expands in proportion to one's courage.
ANAÏS NIN

8

The Law of Resilience

To the one who is victorious and does my will to the end, I will give authority over the nations.

REVELATION 2:26

Revelation 2:26 describes a situation in which those who overcome enormous adversity will be given authority. Power, success, riches . . . all are given as rewards to the winner. It is important to notice that this verse does not refer to professional matters but to faith and salvation. However, we mention it in a figurative way because it is consistent with the Law of Resilience, which says that to get to victory a game must be played, a job must be done, and risks must be taken.

The ability to play the game and take the hard knocks is inherent to good players. In the competitive job market, your employability level rises as your adversity quotient rises. *Adversity quotient* is an expression developed by Paul Stoltz, an American economist, after interviewing over one hundred thousand people to understand why some people make it and others don't.[1]

More significant than the cold and rational intelligence quotient (IQ) and more effective than the psychological evaluation of the emotional quotient (EQ), the adversity quotient (AQ) explains why persistence may be worth more than talent.

Based on his study, Stoltz divided people into three professional groups: climbers, campers, and quitters. Climbers are those who are in search of challenges. They are people who refuse to be insignificant. Quitters, on the other hand, are those who are risk-averse and who look for a comfort zone. And there is a third type: the campers. They are between the climbers and the quitters. They fly the colors but only to a certain point. When risk arises they tend to sit on the wall.

The classification of adversity quotient was created as a way of evaluating how people deal with challenges. Those with a higher AQ do not blame others when problems arise. They know how to take responsibility. They do not see setbacks as obstacles. They accept that problems occur by force of circumstances rather than because of their personal nature.

The Law of Resilience is precisely about knowing how to deal with adversity.

Being resilient is about being able to cope with pressure. The term originates in physics and represents the property of accumulating energy without breaking when pressured or submitted to distress. A good example is when we step on a deep carpet that is squashed but then immediately returns to its normal state after we step off.

In order to pass an exam or to win a race, you need to be resilient and persevere until you reach your goal. That is how you overcome adversity. Many people with greater ability and learning opportunities fail to keep trying and, in the end, give up. There is a Brazilian saying that goes, "In order to pass a test you should not study enough to pass; rather study until you pass." Perseverance is usually more important than financial potential and intelligence.

Knowing how to deal with difficulties is a skill that can be developed. Once again, we have good examples of resilience in the Bible. King David declared, "Even though I walk through the darkest valley, I will fear no evil, for you are with me; your rod and your staff, they comfort me" (Ps. 23:4). No matter what valley you are facing or what size a problem, the Bible teaches you not to despair but instead to have courage, to persevere, and to have confidence and a vision of the possibilities, of triumph, and of hope. David was a great climber: he took on a bear, a lion, and a giant. He had faith that he would overcome the obstacles. Let his example inspire you to overcome hardships.

Learning from Mistakes

> The testing of your faith produces perseverance. Let perseverance finish its work so that you may be mature and complete, not lacking anything. (James 1:3–4)

In the face of problems and adversities, you may experience defeats, setbacks, and failures. Some of these will not necessarily derive from a mistake you have made but may just be part of the game. Not all of our defeats will be due to something we have done; however, it is important to always try to figure out if we could have done something differently and how to be more prepared in the future. The world is changing fast with advances in technology and globalization. We need to keep up.

After failing, some grumble while others learn. As Claus Moller says, "When the winds of change blow, some build shelters and feel secure; others build windmills and get rich."[2] The courage to face up to and learn from problems is one way of becoming more competent.

Crises, defeats, and accidents are part of the learning curve for any company or person. We should not despair in such situations but rather learn from them. As the poet and philosopher Horace said, "Adversity has the effect of eliciting talents which in prosperous circumstances would have lain dormant."

As the authors of this book, we both can testify that our careers were built on defeats. Moreover, everything we achieved was with effort. Our enterprising spirit always made us deal with increasingly greater difficulties, but we never gave in. We always tried to see where we went wrong. Then we would set off to try again. We might have failed again, but not for the same reason.

When it comes to dealing with mistakes, the problem is not the mistake itself but repeating the mistake.

Throughout the journey, we recommend that you follow the lessons of William E. Deming, who speaks of the PDSA (Plan-Do-Study-Act) cycle, in which you plan, do, study the results, and take corrective action at the next attempt, should the first fail.[3] This really works!

This is how the system works: have a plan and try. If you fail, discover what the mistake was and try again, only better. The Neuro-Linguistic Programming (NLP) approach teaches us that we need to know what we want, pay attention to what is happening (the results we obtain), and have the flexibility to change until we get it right.[4] Flexibility is another word for humility. This is the same lesson as the PDSA cycle, only put another way.

This was the lesson we learned from the defeats we suffered: you will never be a loser or a failure—no matter how many setbacks and defeats you experience along the way—provided you stick to your dream, have a good attitude, and keep learning from trial and error. That's how we made it. We challenge you to draw up a strategy to overcome obstacles. Sooner or later you will learn everything you need to make your dream come true.

Don't believe those who criticize your failures or who tell you that you'll never make it. They are negative people, and even if their intentions are good, even if they say it in order to spare you from frustration, they are not people you want to listen to. You need to surround yourself with those who dream with you on the same level, or who at least don't stand in your way. If there is someone who criticizes you and offers good arguments, step back and evaluate what they are saying to see whether there is any truth in it and whether you need to make a change. But give a wide berth to those people who are merely pessimistic.

Keep in mind that the results that will come from your victories will pay back, with interest, the temporary frustration defeat can bring. And every time you face a problem or a crisis, ask yourself: What is this situation trying to teach me?

The great navigators owe their reputation to showers and storms.
EPICURUS

9

The Law of Joy

Do everything without grumbling or arguing.

PHILIPPIANS 2:14

Those who waste their time grumbling miss out on the marvelous effects of the Law of Joy. The Bible expressly mentions: "Rejoice always . . . give thanks in all circumstances" (1 Thess. 5:16) and "Rejoice" (Phil. 4:4). Someone who gives thanks for everything and rejoices always won't be someone who constantly grumbles.

There are people who spend their entire life complaining about what happened to them—what they were missing, what didn't work out, who betrayed them, and so on. These people are incapable of putting a "case closed" stamp on their past. They are incapable of learning the lessons from the setbacks and then moving on. As the old adage goes, when life gives you lemons, make lemonade.

The Reverend Elena Alves Silva of the Methodist University says the following about Esther, the queen of Persia:

There's a story in the Bible that describes the life of Esther. As a girl she was raised by her uncle, after her parents died. She was Jewish and suffered the experience of being removed from her homeland to live in a foreign land. Esther took the throne in the place of Vashti, the previous queen, who was punished with death for not responding to a call from the king, disobeying his orders.

Despite all the adverse circumstances in her life, [Esther] played a central role in the story of the Jewish people, as a heroine and liberator.

The Jews were threatened with death and were involved in a conspiracy organized by Haman, who wanted to see them bowing down and prostrate before him. Esther interceded with the king and ensured that the conspiracy was clarified. Her courage made a difference, because she showed herself to be strong, a true warrior. The end of the story and the victory were celebrated in great style. The tradition remains until present times, in the Jewish holiday of Purim, meaning Day of Luck.

In Esther's story, as in so many other strong women in the Bible, we can draw a lesson: there is no use in complaining about what they have done to us, what matters is knowing that we can make a difference where we are.[1]

Another marvelous case of joy despite circumstances that is worth mentioning is that of Joseph, son of Jacob. Victim of his own brothers' envy, Joseph was sold as a slave and taken to Egypt. There he ended up at Potiphar's home, where he worked and grew to be a person of trust. But Potiphar's wife had other plans. She wanted to have an affair with the young man. Loyal to his boss, Joseph denied the woman's advances, was falsely accused, and was thrown into prison unfairly.

There is no report of Joseph ever having grumbled. In jail, he continued to act nobly and help others. After a while he was released and eventually he became the Egyptian prime minister after predicting a seven-year famine. His story is in the book of Genesis, beginning in chapter 37, and is an excellent case of personal and professional success.

Some say that when God doesn't change the circumstances it's because he wants to change you. In the Bible, Joseph was a victim of injustice and intrigue, but he held on to his ethics and the will to help others. Every step of the way, Joseph was gaining wisdom, increasing in experience, and leaving a positive impression on everyone. Instead of complaining, he took action. Instead of grumbling, he learned. His fate was changed by God's blessing but also by the way he responded to his circumstances.

We all know how irritating it is to work alongside a professional who is constantly whining. Try to avoid being this unpleasant companion.

Start by doing what is necessary, then do what is possible, and suddenly you're doing the impossible.
St. Francis of Assisi

10

The Law of Recharging

Six days do your work, but on the seventh day do not
work, so that your ox and your donkey may rest, and so
that the slave born in your household and the foreigner
living among you may be refreshed.

EXODUS 23:12

When you properly apply the spiritual Law of Recharging by allow-
ing time for leisure and recovery, you will substantially boost your
emotional and physical energy for your work. The Bible strongly
recommends one of the most important means of increasing productivity, but this principle is often seen as a prohibition instead of
useful advice. We are referring to the right to rest communicated
in the Ten Commandments.

Domenico De Masi, an Italian sociologist, raised a revolutionary concept of labor that groups together studies, work, and play
in his book *Creative Idleness*.[1] A mind that is free to think is fertile

ground from which good ideas can spring. Leisure, social contact, and games, in De Masi's opinion, prevent the mechanization of labor.

Medical professionals and labor laws also suggest paid weekly time off. This pause reduces absenteeism and increases productivity.

Well, the One who came up with this idea thousands of years ago is also the Creator of the human machine, and he knows perfectly well how to make it work better. The Bible has a rule about rest in the Ten Commandments: after six days of work, take one day of rest (Exod. 20:9–10). It is called the Shabbat. In Leviticus 25:3–5, we see that the Law of Recharging also applies to the land. The biblical schedule is six years of agricultural production and one year of rest.

What appears to be a prohibition is in fact a favor, a freeing advice. *Shabbat* is a Hebrew term that refers to the seventh day of the week, dedicated—in Judaism—to rest (Exod. 20:8–11; 23:12). Today, it is often referred to as "Sabbath." The Sabbath is a challenge for us to break our routine and take a moment of physical and emotional recuperation, in which one can make the most of life, enjoy one's family, and devote oneself to different activities from those undertaken during the workweek.

Unless they break with routine, people will break down sooner or later, and their productivity and motivation will increasingly decline. It's a simple idea: you work six days and rest one. Of course there are many who in addition to working for six days also work on the seventh because they want to better themselves professionally. When this stops being the exception and becomes the rule, problems ensue.

The biblical advice is to work hard without becoming desperate; rest without becoming lazy or irresponsible. The goal is to have a well-balanced, calm life. To achieve this perfect balance the Bible assures you that God is working the night shift. While you are asleep, God works through nature: "He grants sleep to those he loves" (Ps. 127:2). Nature will run its course if you don't fight it.

According to the physical laws, when a person gets the proper amount of sleep he recovers from the day's work, and that recovery helps the person achieve his or her goals the next day. Thus, whether you believe only in biological laws or also in the higher power who developed them—as we do—you will be rewarded. The only thing that you should avoid is bending the laws of physics, aiming to become more productive by not taking enough breaks in your routine.

While we are sleeping our muscles recover and our brain fixes what we learned during the day; the memories are consolidated. Not sleeping the required minimum that your body needs will adversely affect your performance.

Albert Einstein used to sleep ten hours a day and slept for another hour when he had a new idea. Leonardo da Vinci used to wake up early, but reserved fifteen minutes every two hours for a nap. This way he was able to face challenges with a rested mind.[2]

In our lectures we always talk about the "leisure day." Lately we have been receiving a lot of emails and letters from people who had positive outcomes after practicing this advice faithfully, almost as if it were a doctor's prescription. Many discovered they were more productive after taking a weekly pause. With recharged batteries, they were able to improve their work flow without burning the candle at both ends.

The Law of Recharging says to take one day's rest during the week, on whatever day you choose. On this day, you switch off from all your routine commitments and do different things. It's the day when the faithful go to church, but it's also the day to have lunch with your parents or visit a friend or relative. It's the day when you don't turn on your computer or don't frequent your usual places. It's the day to go to the movies or take a trip to the beach or the park. It's the day for useless or silly pastimes, but those you enjoy doing. Indeed it's a day that can be totally and utterly pleasant.

If you feel guilty about rarely seeing your children or visiting your parents or lavishing attention on someone you love, the Law of Recharging can be a way around that. You can use this time to play with your kids, to honor your parents (which is what they want most of all), or to attend to your marriage.

Having a proper Sabbath isn't always easy. It takes a lot of discipline to have an undisciplined day! In our experience, one of the most difficult aspects of doing this is turning off your mind. Taking your mind off work, business, exams, or day-to-day worries is a challenge of herculean proportions. It's relatively easy to discipline yourself not to work, not to read work-related material, and not to turn on the computer. But it is really difficult not to think about these things. If this challenge is overcome, the Shabbat will be even better, and your recovery and increase in performance will be exceptional.

Ways to Recharge

He said to them, "This is what the LORD commanded: 'Tomorrow is to be a day of sabbath *rest*, a holy sabbath to the LORD. So bake what you want to bake and boil what you want to boil. Save whatever is left and keep it until morning.'" (Exod. 16:23, emphasis added)

The Sabbath is a weekly concept, but it can and should have repercussions in other time frames as well.

Once a day, even if it's only five, ten, or fifteen minutes, take a moment to relax. Breathe in, listen to music, observe the landscape, or enjoy a painting or a pretty photograph. Think about your life, be grateful for everything you have lived and learned, and appreciate what you have. Recall the good things that happen to you every day or reflect upon a very special moment of your life.

Two to three times a week, engage in physical activity. You can walk with your spouse, a friend, or your dog; run while listening to music you like; or cycle indoors while reading about a topic you need to learn. Physical activity releases endorphins, a natural stimulant and antidepressant. It does your body and soul good and improves your mood. It also helps prevent obesity, heart attacks, and strokes. Physical activity can be done on your day of rest but should be done more than once a week.

Once a month, have a very different day. You will probably use your weekly day of rest for this; that is okay as long as you do something different from your usual routine. Visit a tourist attraction close to you where you have never gone with your family. As residents of the Rio de Janeiro region, we are always surprised by the number of locals who have never been to the Sugarloaf Cable Car, climbed up to the statue of Christ the Redeemer at the peak of the Corcovado mountain, gone to the Planetarium of Gávea, or visited the city zoo. These are simple and affordable activities that can become very special, magical moments for you and whomever you take with you. That's how the best things in life usually are: simple.

Once a year, usually on a national holiday or while on vacation, use your imagination for something really different, like a trip. If you have some money in savings, maybe now is the time to enjoy Bora Bora Island. If money is an issue, enjoy what is available locally. Many people fail to enjoy what they have or go where they want because they focus on what they don't have. Be creative and think of something interesting. Some may use that trip to Paris or Bora Bora as motivation to keep studying and working. This normally works and it really pays off when you get there. Another idea is to try using these days to simply stay home, without doing anything—no travel obligations and no fancy programs. Sometimes a few days at home doing nothing can be the best of fun.

Simplicity is the ultimate sophistication.
Leonardo DaVinci

PART 3

Laws concerning Values

11

The Law of Self-Hiring

Many claim to have unfailing love, but a faithful person
who can find?

PROVERBS 20:6

Let's begin with a test: Would you hire yourself to be your employee? Would you like to be the business partner of someone just like you? This is the Law of Self-Hiring. You know yourself inside out, what you are capable of, your dedication, and so on. Don't give a quick answer to these questions or an acceptable one just for the sake of it. Think about them, be honest with yourself, and then answer. If you wouldn't hire yourself, then why do you think someone else would? If you went to work for someone, time would reveal your qualities and flaws.

There are many people who spend the majority of their leisure time watching TV, browsing social networks, or participating in chat rooms. Research conducted among rich and successful people has shown that the higher the level of professional excellence, the

87

less time spent watching TV.[1] It's easy to understand that rising to the top requires devotion and preparation. Achieving success is difficult. Staying there is even harder. Do you have the devotion and balance necessary to justify hiring you?

Quite often we (the authors) recommend people for a job only to find out afterward that the person's opportunity to work (or to go back to work) didn't last long. The person got the job but didn't work properly; he or she was lazy or incompetent, disagreeable, or even dishonest. And of course the person lost the job while we, on the other hand, ended up frustrated. We had also been put in a tight spot with those who trusted our recommendation.

There's no use in being introduced by someone, getting a chance, and then not being a good professional. In fact, your work ethic and your accomplishments are the best way to introduce yourself to someone. Here is William's statement on the matter:

> At one time I was a teacher at the Fluminense Federal University (UFF-RJ). Professors were poorly paid, the atmosphere was discouraging, and performance was low overall, with many absences and delays on the part of the professors. But I had a job to do and I did it. I arrived at the correct time. I provided good classes, and I was demanding when it came to exams. I ended up teaching at a private university because the owner, after seeing me teach, invited me to earn a bit more as a professor and work for him. So I quit my job at UFF and joined a private university. I made substantial progress in my professional career and my salary because I was doing my job properly.

When you do your job properly you have a better chance of keeping it or getting a better one. New opportunities always present themselves to good professionals, and you'll have the option of choosing the best one.

For years we have observed and tried to put together how employability works and how to make money. We always found it odd that employers looking for professionals in the marketplace would say they were difficult to find while, at the same time, unemployed professionals would say how difficult it was to find a job. Something is not quite right in this scenario! How can it be that companies are complaining about the lack of good employees, while employees are complaining about the scarcity of good jobs? You know what's wrong? There is a lack of trained people in the market. Right now Brazil is experiencing a shortage of qualified manpower and is trying to fix that by importing a specialized workforce from other countries.

We will say it again: if you are properly prepared or focused on bettering yourself, if you are reliable and hardworking, we are quite sure that good opportunities will come your way. Companies increasingly need professionals who are respectable, honest, productive, committed, and assertive. The more good qualities you can attain, the more people will seek you out.

These characteristics go beyond your résumé and your job interview. The job market has to attribute these qualities to you. Obtaining this credibility and public acknowledgment takes time and requires us to overcome difficult and sometimes humiliating circumstances.

You might think we are asking too much and that it is impossible to have all these characteristics, but take a moment to consider whether you yourself would not seek them when hiring someone. From now on your challenge is to become someone you would hire. The more you distinguish yourself from the average person (in a good way, of course!), the higher your chances of success. Therefore, get moving!

Discipline is the bridge between goals and accomplishment.
JIM ROHN

12

The Law of Honesty

You shall not steal.

EXODUS 20:15; DEUTERONOMY 5:19

Integrity has several dimensions, but nothing sums it up better than honesty. It is one of the three basic pillars of success, together with wisdom/competence and energy/willingness. Being honest involves a range of attitudes and behaviors.

To be honest one cannot be a slave to money. These slaves end up closing bad deals. As a federal judge, William is tired of convicting people who tried to make money in an easy and improper way by becoming involved in larceny and fraud. Today they are in prison.

The kind of money that brings prosperity comes from work, and it brings with it the recognition of those around us. In Brazil, illegal money ends up being the snitch of those who have it, whether it is traced by the authorities, such as the courts or the attorney general's office, the Financial Activities Control Board (COAFI), the Federal

Bank, the police, or even through the perception of society itself, which judges the behavior of its members.

The Ten Commandments, for example, are clear in their recommendations regarding basic economic issues: don't steal, don't lie, and don't covet. In other words, instead of coveting what others have, go fix your own life.

Here are a few questions to ask yourself in order to gauge whether you are being honest:

Do your actions go against the laws of your country?

Could all your endeavors be filmed or published without bringing shame to you or leading to criminal or civil prosecution?

If others did the same to you, would you be pleased?

Would you do the same to someone you love?

Is someone being harmed or swindled because of your actions? (In other words, is anyone facing exaggerated losses while you make exaggerated profits?)

If what you are doing or negotiating passes the above tests with flying colors, then congratulations—keep going! If not, be careful, for the Law of Sowing, which we'll discuss in a later chapter, is inexorable. If something goes wrong, don't blame God or the devil, temptation, the government, or the rain. Take responsibility for your actions and choices—another principle of success.

The matter of honesty is so serious that the Bible leaves no room even for behaviors permitted in law if they oppress those in need. In the words of Isaiah: "Woe to those who make unjust laws, to those who issue oppressive decrees, to deprive the poor of their rights and withhold justice from the oppressed of my people, making widows their prey and robbing the fatherless" (10:1–2).

There is a popular saying in Brazil, "If the rascal knew how profitable it is to be honest, he would be honest just to get the upper hand." This basically means that the person who benefits the most from your honesty is yourself.

Warren Buffett gives the following advice: "In looking for people to hire, you look for three qualities: integrity, intelligence, and energy. And if you don't have the first, the other two will kill you. You think about it; it's true. If you hire somebody without [integrity], you really want them to be dumb and lazy."[1] In other words, in order to succeed you need honesty, competence, and hard work. This principle is supported by research from Robert Half Management Resources. The study titled "Honesty Still the Best Policy: CFO Survey Finds Integrity Most Desired Leadership Quality" (May 31, 2007) found that three-fourths of workers cited integrity as a top attribute of corporate leaders.[2]

For those of you who believe that crime pays off, take a look at the most and least corrupt countries in the world according to the NGO Transparency International and you'll discover a principle at work. The index lists 180 countries and is based on the perception of professionals and analysts of the degree of corruption and runs from one—the most corrupt—to ten—the least corrupt, or the face of honesty. Below are the ten most and the ten least corrupt nations in the world:

Most Corrupt

1	Somalia	1.0
2	North Korea	1.0
3	Myanmar	1.5
4	Afghanistan	1.5
5	Uzbekistan	1.6
6	Turkmenistan	1.6

92

7	Sudan	1.6
8	Iraq	1.8
9	Haiti	1.8
10	Venezuela	1.9

Least Corrupt

1	New Zealand	9.5
2	Denmark	9.4
3	Finland	9.4
4	Sweden	9.3
5	Singapore	9.2
6	Norway	9.0
7	Holland	8.9
8	Australia	8.8
9	Switzerland	8.8
10	Canada	8.7

Brazil is in seventy-third place, with a score of 3.8 in the global ranking. The United States is in twenty-fourth place, with a score of 7.1.[3]

It doesn't take much to notice that the more developed countries with the highest quality of life and life expectancy are more honest. One could argue that the reason for this is that in more developed countries, people don't have to commit fraud. We believe, however, that the reason these countries have developed is precisely because of low corruption. In other words, honesty is not a consequence but rather one of the causes of development.

Brazil's corruption index is still very high, and that is one of the reasons our home country has a low level of development. Imagine how much more developed Brazil would be if we changed our cultural practice of "always finding a way around something" and "always having the upper hand" and moved in the direction of high standards and honest work.

The Higher Degree of Honesty

> [Teach workers] not to steal from [their employers], but to show
> that they can be fully trusted. (Titus 2:10)

There are levels of honesty and of dishonesty. On one level,
being honest means respecting the law and fulfilling your contracts.
However, the Bible also tells us not to cheat anyone. This is the Law
of Honesty applied at a higher level.

Cheating people is abusing them—taking advantage of their
weakness, naiveté, or inferior position. We live in a world where
many people say that you have to have the upper hand to make
the biggest profit.

In the Bible, we see laws broken and people cheated. For example, the prophet Amos says,

> Hear this, you who trample the needy
>   and do away with the poor of the land,
> saying,
> "When will the New Moon be over
>   that we may sell grain,
> and the Sabbath be ended
>   that we may market wheat?"—
> skimping on the measure,
>   boosting the price
>   and cheating with dishonest scales,
> buying the poor with silver
>   and the needy for a pair of sandals,
>   selling even the sweepings with the wheat. (8:4–6)

In this passage we see explicit dishonesty in the reduction of
measures, the use of crooked scales, the mixing of materials (such

as adding chaff, or "sweepings," to the wheat), and the inflating of prices, resulting in people being cheated and taken advantage of. Dishonest practices also stain one's reputation: "People curse the one who hoards grain, but they pray God's blessing on the one who is willing to sell" (Prov. 11:26).

Oftentimes we have to deal with gray areas where a moral or ethical issue is at stake. When these types of situations arise, we may find ourselves in a difficult position.

For example, let's say that by accident an employee from a maintenance company sends an incorrect price quote with an unrealistically low estimation. The client notices the mistake, but instead of pointing it out, he demands that the company abide by that estimation. Legally the client may be right, but morally and ethically he is breaking the "do not cheat" principle. People who take advantage of the vulnerabilities of others are going against the Law of Honesty.

Obeying the law and respecting a contract are not enough. You also can't take advantage of people and situations to reap excessive profits. The Bible warns us, "Woe to him who builds his palace by unrighteousness, his upper rooms by injustice, making his own people work for nothing, not paying them for their labor" (Jer. 22:13).

By being honest and acting properly you may earn less at first, but you will be respected and this is far better. Jorge Ziegler, a Brazilian businessman, told us the following story. A truck driver, after filling his tank at a gas station, asked the clerk if he could issue an invoice with a different price. This is a common type of fraud that allows the driver to keep the difference between the sum paid and the total that he will later ask to be refunded. The clerk replied negatively to the proposal. Irritated, the truck driver asked to talk to the manager, since it was a common practice and all other gas stations were willing to oblige. Ziegler, who was on site, jumped to back the clerk and told the truck driver that he would rather lose him as a client than do something dishonest.

A couple of months later the man returned to the gas station. He introduced himself as the owner of a large shipping company, and he had been checking up on gas stations in the region. Based on Ziegler's ethical posture, the owner had determined that his drivers would, from now on, fuel their trucks only at his gas station when they were in the region.

This is why you should always choose the honest road. If you are facing a situation in which you are not sure what to do, do what is honest and right. If the choice is to look like a fool, choose to be a fool.

A good indication that something is dishonest is that feeling that "something is not right." If it looks or sounds fishy, there is a good bet that it is indeed fishy. In any case, heed the advice given by the apostle Paul: "Reject every kind of evil" (1 Thess. 5:22). Avoiding dubious attitudes and actions will keep you from getting into trouble.

The Power of Words

> All you need to say is simply "Yes" or "No"; anything beyond this comes from the evil one. (Matt. 5:37)

Honesty includes telling the truth. In other words, it means your word is your bond, and this will reflect on your credibility. Jesus tells us that our words should be yes or no, meaning that we should not swear by someone else or make excuses or find scapegoats. As we all know, lies don't travel far, and when revealed they tend to stain the reputation of the perpetrator.

Many people try to cover up a mistake, a problem, or an uncomfortable situation with lies and deceit, regardless of the fact that this will stain their reputation. The Bible shows the harmful effects of lying: "Food gained by fraud tastes sweet, but one ends up with a mouth full of gravel" (Prov. 20:17).

Honesty is one of life's cornerstone values. It is important to the image you project, your relationships, and your career. Maintain high levels of honesty. Do not cheat your neighbor. Do not exploit others. This is advice given by both venture capitalists and scholars, and this spiritual law is also part of the wisdom of the Bible.

> *Then some soldiers asked him, "And what should we do?" He replied, "Don't extort money and don't accuse people falsely—be content with your pay."*
> LUKE 3:14

13

The Law of Names

A good name is more desirable than great riches.

PROVERBS 22:1

Your name is your greatest professional asset. Therefore, the Law of Names is one of the most important spiritual laws for a successful personal career or company.

There is always someone willing to compromise on principles and values in order to achieve success and material goods. In our opinion, this exchange isn't worth it, as stated in Proverbs 22:1. Your name—in other words, your credibility and reputation—is your greatest asset. A professional's name is the most important reference point for his or her career. Your name may or may not signify dignity, high added value, and positive differentials. We say this from our own experience, because during our careers we have observed that those who sacrifice their values—their personal honor, integrity, and honesty—in exchange for a rapid rise in life pay a very high price. Some do indeed achieve significant results, but success is short-lived or comes at an unacceptable cost.

"Time takes vengeance on the matters that are done without its collaboration," says Eduardo Couture, a Brazilian law scholar.[1] The passage of time reveals the character of an individual's name and of the person bearing it. All you have to do is wait. Abraham Lincoln famously said, "You can fool all the people some of the time, and some of the people all the time, but you cannot fool all the people all the time."[2]

The Bible says, "There is nothing concealed that will not be disclosed, or hidden that will not be made known" (Luke 12:2). So don't think you'll get far without meeting the requisite of a "good name," and don't think you'll achieve 100 percent success by hiding something you did in order to rise in the world.

When applied to corporations, the Law of Names becomes the Law of Branding, a concept studied by Adilson Romualdo Neves, author of *Qualidade no Atendimento* (roughly translated as *Quality service*).[3] According to Neves, the Law of Branding refers to the process used to measure the consumer's perception of a product or company. In an article published by the large management consulting group *Instituto Jetro*, Neves explains that the science of branding uses concepts of marketing, administration, architecture, design, advertisement, anthropology, psychology, sociology, and a number of other fields to structure a company's brand for its clients. "It is a way of building and managing a brand using all the interaction points between the company and its clients,"[4] he says, quoting Jane Pavitt, a professor at Princeton University for whom "branding is ultimately the association process of a name and a reputation."[5]

These concepts can easily be applied to people and the image presented to society.

What If I Have Already Made a Mistake?

Whoever conceals their sins does not prosper, but the one who confesses and renounces them finds mercy. (Prov. 28:13)

Ideally, you should always do the right thing, but if you have made a mistake, we recommend that you make amends as quickly as possible. We have witnessed cases in which an employee made a mistake and chose to come clean rather than wait until his boss found out. This attitude worked in his favor, creating trust and avoiding more serious consequences, such as being fired. Bosses know that everyone makes mistakes but that loyalty and sincerity are rare qualities.

The next time you have an opportunity to close a deal, remember Solomon's teachings regarding the value of your name (Prov. 22:1), and you will have a guideline by which to evaluate how to behave. Let go of the illusion of easy money. Never cheat someone. If you do, be assured that, as we say in Brazil, "Time is the lord of truth." In other words, all truth will be revealed in due time.

Among honorable people your word is enough. When you enjoy this degree of credibility, when your word is worth more than a signed document, then your professional path is set toward success. There is a degree of trust that dispenses with documents and signatures. It's good to negotiate with honorable people. In fact, when someone is honest, no contract is needed; when they aren't honest, a contract is not much of a guarantee. However, the best thing is to put business contracts on paper; do it whenever possible.

Among those true to their word, paper is used to recall what was agreed, and if one of the parties should die, the family too will know what had been agreed.

A good name requires honesty but not honesty alone. It requires attention to detail, seriousness, and professional dedication. Maintaining your good name demands constant surveillance. Imagine a professor who begins teaching things that are not true or not backed by research or thought. He will be destroying his greatest asset. However, when someone routinely practices good behavior in order to protect his or her name and reputation, this becomes a habit that breeds success.

The Law of Names works for everyone—bosses, employees, doctors, freelancers, and so on.

Honesty, Credibility, and Profits

Turn from evil and do good; seek peace and pursue it. (Ps. 34:14)

In the late 1990s a study evaluated the relationship between car manufacturers and suppliers in three countries: Japan, South Korea, and the United States. The lead researchers were Jeffrey Dyer, a professor from the University of Pennsylvania, and Wujin Chu, a professor from Seoul National University. The analysis of 453 negotiations revealed that the transaction costs of negotiating with the least trustworthy companies were considerably higher than those with the most reliable. Time and money spent on the negotiations and regulations were five times higher in these cases. With the most reliable companies, information was shared and the results improved. There was a willingness to go that extra mile.[6]

Harvard researchers found an even more direct relationship between trust and profits. They monitored sixty-five hundred employees from the seventy-six hotels in the Holiday Inn chain in the United States and Canada. The hotels where employees trusted management's promises and values were more profitable than those where there was a lack of trust by the staff. The connection between trust/credibility and profit was "so strong that a one-eighth point improvement in a hotel's score [on a scale of zero to five] could be expected to increase the hotel profitability by 2.5% of revenues," affirmed Tony Simons in the *Harvard Business Review*. "No other single aspect of manager behavior that we measured had as large an impact on profits."[7]

> *It takes twenty years to build a reputation and five minutes to ruin it. If you think about that, you'll do things differently.*
> WARREN BUFFETT

14

The Law of the Company You Keep

Do not be misled: "Bad company corrupts good character."

1 Corinthians 15:33

Let's talk about the Law of the Company You Keep. We gave this spiritual principle this name to simplify a far-reaching concept. In Brazil, our mothers used to say, "You can't root with hogs and have a clean nose." This is similar to the American saying, "Birds of a feather flock together." This is the truth. Rarely can someone belong to a group and, if in the minority, influence the group more than the person is influenced by it. People tend to band together, which is why people say, "You are only as good as the company you keep."

Perhaps you're asking yourself why this law isn't included in part 4, which will deal with spiritual laws concerning relationships.

Indeed, it wouldn't be out of place there, but we have included it here as a spiritual law concerning values in order to stress that the company you keep influences your behavior, your integrity, and your image. Even if you aren't influenced to do something wrong, if you keep bad company you will be associated with them.

Therefore, if you want to advance your career, surround yourself with those who are positive role models—who share the same dreams and values.

This law applies not only to your day-to-day circle of friends but also to those with whom you do business. Warren Buffett can teach us a thing or two here. He has been named by *Forbes* magazine as the third richest man on the planet, with a fortune estimated at fifty billion dollars. Buffett owns Berkshire Hathaway, one of the world's most respected investment firms. He has already donated forty billion dollars to philanthropic institutions. In terms of cash donations, he's considered one of the greatest philanthropists in the history of mankind. Buffett has also led other millionaires to support charitable causes, which is highly commendable. Here is what this rich, intelligent man has to say about the company you keep: "You can't make a good deal with a bad person."[1]

One of the greatest financial investors in the history of the planet advises us not to do business with dishonest or bad people. We are not talking about religious prejudice, nor are we saying that you should not ever do business with unbelievers. Instead, we are merely agreeing with Warren Buffett in advising that if you want to get ahead in life, you should connect with those who enjoy working, are aboveboard, and have good sense. When honorable professionals get together, they create synergy and a circle of virtue that mutually strengthen one another.

So we'll conclude with two pieces of advice:

1. Don't do business with bad people.
2. Don't be the bad guy with whom the good guys shouldn't do business!

Avoid Bad Company

He who walks with wise men will be wise, but the companion of fools will suffer harm. (Prov. 13:20)

"But aren't you proposing segregation?" you may be asking. Not at all. Not doing business with bad people is exercising your personal choice, to which we are all entitled.

Of course, there's nothing preventing you from having a relationship with those you love, even if they are not on the right path. You can even try to help them see the advantages of following these spiritual laws, joining the crowd of hard workers who study and abide by positive values. But remember: each of us chooses what we want for ourselves. You cannot choose for someone else; you can only make your own choices.

With love and respect, without arrogance or cruelty, you can caution those who have taken the wrong road. In that vein the Bible says, "But if you do warn the wicked person to turn from their ways and they do not do so, they will die for their sin, though you yourself will be saved" (Ezek. 33:9). The Bible also says, "We urge you, brothers and sisters, warn those who are idle and disruptive, encourage the disheartened, help the weak, be patient with everyone" (1 Thess. 5:14).

Avoiding the influence of the wrong people is an important spiritual principle that contributes to success. We must also avoid situations in which we could be compared with others and be wary of people who depend on or exploit their friends, relatives, or colleagues. These people are like relational vampires who are always feeding off the success of others.

Be cautious when, for emotional or humanitarian reasons, you try to help bad people or the wrong type of company. If you feel you are being influenced more than you are influencing, distance yourself. And please don't confuse helping others with becoming involved with them or their situations. Helping others is a good thing, but never hire someone or become a business partner with the wrong person just to be helpful. Businesses and partnerships should be made in an objective and intelligent manner. If you want to be a philanthropist, that is fine—set up a healthy business with competent people who can commit to the company and make money. And then, with the money you earn, go ahead and help others.

Blessed is the one who does not walk in step with the wicked or stand in the way that sinners take or sit in the company of mockers, but whose delight is in the law of the LORD, and who meditates on his law day and night. That person is like a tree planted by streams of water, which yields its fruit in season and whose leaf does not wither—whatever they do prospers.

PSALM 1:1–3

15

The Law of Self-Control

Better a patient person than a warrior, one with self-control than one who takes a city.

PROVERBS 16:32

In order to apply all the spiritual laws listed in this book, but especially in order to be a righteous person, it is fundamental that you learn the Law of Self-Control.

Napoleon Hill, when writing about self-control—a feature he said was common to all successful men—states that having self-control is in fact being your own man. It means thinking in the long-term, appraising the consequences of every action, understanding how what you do either leads you nearer to or distances you from the main objective you have set for yourself. He also claims that "a man who is bound by the slavery of debt has no time or inclination to set up or work out ideals, with the result that he drifts downward with time until he eventually begins to set up limitations in his own mind, and by these he hedges himself behind prison walls of fear and doubt from which he never escapes."[1]

In the Bible, Paul also teaches us about self-control:

> Do you not know that in a race all the runners run, but only one gets the prize? Run in such a way as to get the prize. Everyone who competes in the games goes into strict training. They do it to get a crown that will not last, but we do it to get a crown that will last forever. Therefore I do not run like someone running aimlessly; I do not fight like a boxer beating the air. No, I strike a blow to my body and make it my slave so that after I have preached to others, I myself will not be disqualified for the prize. (1 Cor. 9:24–27)

To achieve a dream, a goal, or a victory, you should:

- run like a winner ("in such a way as to get the prize");
- make sacrifices (go into "strict training");
- have faith and trust ("not . . . running aimlessly");
- behave in an intelligent and objective way ("not fight like a boxer beating the air"); and
- take charge of yourself and have self-control ("strike a blow to my body and make it my slave").

Learning to control your mind, your body, and your time is to be in control of yourself. Those who don't control themselves first are in no condition to control anything else.

Become Vigilant

For whatever is hidden is meant to be disclosed. (Mark 4:22)

One thing that must be remembered is that, in the corporate world, you are being observed. Everything you do, as well as what you say, give, and receive, is being observed by others and may be used either for you or against you. We are not talking about appearances but rather attitudes and actions, how you behave around and communicate with others.

How you behave professionally cannot be separated from the rest of your relationships, including how you are as a friend and a spouse, as an employee or business partner, as a parent, a child, a citizen, a student, and so on. It's worth remembering that people often behave differently in good times than in moments of adversity, but in both cases there is someone watching.

The Bible states, "In everything set them an example by doing what is good. In your teaching show integrity, seriousness and soundness of speech that cannot be condemned, so that those who oppose you may be ashamed because they have nothing bad to say" about you (Titus 2:7–8). And in this passage of spiritual advice, "those who oppose you" includes anyone who doesn't know you well, anyone who could have the intention of acting maliciously toward you if given the opportunity, anyone who hopes you won't be successful. It's better to live in such a way that you have nothing that you fear being exposed by your enemies.

The best lesson we can learn is to do "what is good" not only when others are watching but also when no one is watching. "Obey them not only to win their favor when their eye is on you, but as slaves of Christ, doing the will of God from your heart" (Eph. 6:6).

Therefore, if you want to be successful in any endeavor, be aware of your behavior and make sure that all of your actions are ethical, righteous, and professional. Behave as if you are being videotaped.

Don't be overly critical or lazy or the type who has an answer for everything. Do be the one who provides good service to your customers and your boss; be pleasant. The Brazilian expression "Good men do not complain" is an excellent one. Most people do not regret keeping their mouth shut.

The safest way to practice the Law of Self-Control is by not doing anything that might adversely affect your trustworthiness. Think about yourself: Are you trustworthy? Do you keep your word and meet your deadlines? Do you deliver what you promised? Or better yet, do you deliver more than what was requested or promised? Do you go the extra mile? Do you treat your customer, your boss or business partner, and your coworkers the same way you would like to be treated? Your answers will demonstrate your level of self-control, and self-control will pave your road to success.

To be known for your honesty and integrity is vital if you want to be respected as a professional and earn self-respect. People who lack principles don't always sleep well at night, because deep down they know it is wrong to act dishonestly.

Avoid Oversharing in the Workplace

> Like a city whose walls are broken through is a person who lacks self-control. (Prov. 25:28)

Practicing self-control is one of the best forms of self-protection you can have. When you allow someone too much intimacy, you are setting the perimeter for future trouble. There are those who pour their hearts out at work. They talk about everything that is going on in their personal lives; they overshare and congratulate themselves for being sincere and honest. This is a mistake that can jeopardize your career.

There is a proper place for everything. Your coworker is not necessarily your friend and doesn't need to know the details of your personal life. Likewise, you should avoid knowing the details of your coworkers' personal lives. Your work environment is not your home or club or group therapy session. Stay on a need-to-know basis with your colleagues.

This doesn't mean you are cold, standoffish, or indifferent to others' feelings and circumstances. And it goes without saying that you shouldn't be antisocial. Be courteous and genuinely interested in others but draw some lines. Healthy boundaries between your work and your personal life will keep the problems out.

Regarding this issue of self-control and personal boundaries, Solomon's advice is in order: "Fools find no pleasure in understanding but delight in airing their own opinions" (Prov. 18:2). It is foolish to become the center of attention. It is better to be interested in others' opinions and thoughts. If you value and listen to others, you will be seen as a nice, easygoing person. You can also learn from others, especially if you take our advice and follow the Law of the Company You Keep, which urges you to be selective regarding the people with whom you choose to surround yourself.

Don't overshare but be willing to build healthy professional relationships. Draw lines, not walls. As the saying goes, "Good fences make good neighbors," which doesn't mean alienating people in your day-to-day life but keeping everything in its proper place. In this sense, Joseph Fort Newton had it right: "People are lonely because they build walls instead of bridges."[2] There are good and bad walls. When it comes to your professional success, choose wisely the ones you are going to build and the ones you are going to tear down.

> *Do not repay anyone evil for evil. Be careful to*
> *do what is right in the eyes of everyone.*
> Romans 12:17

PART 4

Laws concerning Relationships

16

The Law of Love

"Teacher, which is the greatest commandment in the
Law?" Jesus replied: "'Love the Lord your God with
all your heart and with all your soul and with all your
mind.' This is the first and greatest commandment.
And the second is like it: 'Love your neighbor as yourself.' All the Law and the Prophets hang on these two
commandments."

MATTHEW 22:36–40

Loving your neighbor is a good starting point for interpersonal
and social relationships. Doing so will be reflected in the manner
in which you treat your neighbor and how you value him or her.
The concept of loving your neighbor seems rather idealistic, but
there are many practical and successful applications of this concept.

How did Gandhi beat the British army and set India free without firing a single shot? How did Martin Luther King Jr., with an

equally nonviolent movement, manage to revolutionize civil rights in the United States? And what about Nelson Mandela? How did he manage to end apartheid in South Africa? Each of these leaders resorted to a very powerful spiritual law: the Law of Love.

In applying this law, these leaders implemented the concepts of nonviolent, peaceful resistance and civil disobedience. This powerful spiritual law produced concrete results that most people considered impossible to obtain. How could unarmed citizens with no military training overcome police and military forces as well as their enemies? Armed only with their spiritual principles, Gandhi, Martin Luther King Jr., and Nelson Mandela won their wars.

With his campaign of nonviolence and love, Dr. King became one of the most important leaders of the civil rights movement in the United States and the entire world. He was the youngest person to be awarded, in 1964, the Nobel Prize. A brilliant speaker, Dr. King faced a lot of hatred, which led to his assassination in April 1968. Here is an impressive excerpt from one of his sermons.

[To] our most bitter opponents [we] say: "We shall match your capacity to inflict suffering by our capacity to endure suffering. We will meet your physical force with soul force. Do to us what you will and we will still love you. We cannot in all good conscience obey your unjust laws, . . . because noncooperation with evil is as much a moral obligation as is cooperation with good, and so throw us in jail and we will still love you. Bomb our homes and threaten our children, and . . . we will still love you. Send your hooded perpetrators of violence into our communities at the midnight hour and . . . leave us half dead as you beat us, and we will still love you. . . . But be assured that we'll wear you down by our capacity to suffer, and one day we will win our freedom. We will not only win freedom for ourselves; we will so appeal to your heart and conscience that we will win you in the process, and our victory will be a double victory."[1]

Doing good to those who present us with evil is worth it. Jesus says to a crowd of followers: "You have heard that it was said, 'Love your neighbor and hate your enemy.' But I tell you, love your enemies and pray for those who persecute you" (Matt. 5:43–44). For many people, loving, forgiving, and praying for your enemies is almost impossible. The idea itself can be overwhelming. But think for a second: a person who harms no one is more likely to turn enemies into friends and make a positive impression on others. Hence, the Law of Love works.

Similar advice is given by Solomon in the Old Testament and repeated by the apostle Paul in the New Testament: "If your enemy is hungry, give him food to eat; if he is thirsty, give him water to drink" (Prov. 25:21; see also Rom. 12:20). When we do good things to those who harm us, we give them no choice but to change their behavior. Either they change their ways, or they find themselves in the hot seat, at least in front of others. Normally our good actions toward them will make them aware of their harmful attitudes toward us.

The Golden Rule

So in everything, do to others what you would have them do to you, for this sums up the Law and the Prophets. (Matt. 7:12)

The Golden Rule recommends that we treat others as we would want them to treat us. This is one of the simplest yet most effective principles in the world—treat others as you would like to be treated. Imagine what the world would be like if managers treated their employees as they would want to be treated, and vice versa. Or if every company offered their customers the same level of service they would like to receive. What if Wall Street traders treated investors with the same loyalty they would desire if on the other side of the transaction? Or public servants treated the public with the same care they would like? What if competitors practiced the Golden Rule?

Of course this revolutionary concept is not applicable to the workplace alone. Every human interaction could benefit from it. What if spouses treated each other in this manner, as well as parents, children, and neighbors? Would people be more tolerant? Would they respect one another more?

The lesson taught by Jesus in Galilee was also confirmed in a study by Napoleon Hill that presents the Golden Rule as doing unto others what we would like them to do to us if we were in their shoes.

Hill understood that the Golden Rule is a very efficient law when it comes to professional success. He suggests:

> You can comprehend this law quite easily by regarding yourself as a sort of human magnet that attracts those whose characters harmonize with your own. In thus regarding yourself as a magnet that attracts to you all who harmonize with your dominating characteristics and repels all who do not so harmonize, you should keep in mind, also, the fact that you are the builder of that magnet; also, that you may change its nature so that it will correspond to any ideal that you may wish to set up and follow. And, most important of all, you should keep in mind the fact that this entire process of change takes place through thought![2]

However, more than attracting people, the Law of Love—demonstrated through the Golden Rule—benefits those who follow it. As each person's career and business are the direct result of human interactions, special advantages will accrue to those who are pleasant and agreeable, whose attitudes make them the kind of person or company that others want to be around.

Appreciating Others

Just as a body, though one, has many parts, but all its many parts form one body, so it is with Christ. (1 Cor. 12:12)

Every person, every function, and every job is worthy. Unfortunately not everybody sees things this way. There is no unimportant or less honorable job. In order to function, society needs everyone to play his or her part. As the apostle Paul says, "Our presentable parts need no special treatment. But God has put the body together, giving greater honor to the parts that lacked it, so that there should be no division in the body, but that its parts should have equal concern for each other. If one part suffers, every part suffers with it; if one part is honored, every part rejoices with it" (1 Cor. 12:24–26).

The bottom line is this: all parts of the body are important. What would happen if your foot or your hand decided it wasn't important and wanted instead to become a head? How would your body function with a couple of heads in command? The body needs the head, but it also needs the feet to give balance and the hands to reach for things. The same idea works in a team, a department, or a company. For that reason, we should value and appreciate all people, regardless of their position in society or the company's hierarchy.

Back in fifteenth-century England, King Richard III, facing the most dreadful battle of his life, stated, "A horse, a horse! My kingdom for a horse!" The quote became popular in the hands of William Shakespeare[3] and means that there are moments when even being the king isn't enough. Sometimes your power and riches simply can't give you what you need; you need the help of others.

In the board game of life, each piece has its value. Whatever the role a person has to play, it should be applauded. Even if your part is a simple one, be proud of it and do it well.

There are those who don't move forward because they think less of themselves. They assume they are unable to do anything of value or significance. Each and every one of us, no matter our position, can improve our station in life if we want to. If you feel fulfilled where you are, don't try to change simply to please society.

The idea is quite simple: value your neighbor and value yourself. Think about every single member of the team. Love your neighbor as you love yourself.

The measure of love is to love without measure.
SAINT AUGUSTINE

17

The Law of Agreement

Do two walk together unless they have agreed to do so?

AMOS 3:3

The Law of Agreement involves seeking healthy and friendly relationships, avoiding unnecessary battles and litigation, and acting as a peacemaker wherever you are. Agreement is necessary even with your enemies, and even more so with your spouse, family, business partners, customers, and suppliers. Agreements serve not just to avoid problems but also to create something fundamental: your relationship network. Many people forget that when others collaborate with us, our chances of success are greater.

Specialists point to three fundamental stages in personal and professional development: dependence, independence, and interdependence. Early in life, either as a baby or when starting a career, we are totally dependent on those around us. In the next stage, as a teenager or a recently promoted employee, we become independent in our basic tasks. We know what to do in most situations. Finally, as adults or high-end professionals, we reach the most advanced stage: interdependence. At this stage, a person knows how much they need others and how much others need them.

Only those who understand the Law of Agreement—those who are cooperative and seek the cooperation of others—make it to the top and remain there. When there is agreement, there is synergy and a virtuous cycle of mutual development.

Within the context of building relationships, we must learn how to get along with all types of people and how to overcome our differences. There are those who say, "I won't turn the other cheek." These people are always ready to fight and unwilling to forgive or come to an agreement. But a willingness to forgive and compromise are important characteristics in those who seek professional and personal success.

In law, whenever there is a conflict, the courts tend to strive toward consensus. Attorneys in Brazil have a saying: "A bad deal is better than a good fight." Arbitrators and judges are compelled to work out agreements in many controversies that come to court, and should they fail, the penalty is to have the case dismissed. Legislators have taken this precaution to avoid stretching out conflicts that cost both parties and the state time and money.

Similarly, diplomacy is a mechanism for discussing interests and avoiding conflict between foreign states. International organizations and regional blocs strive to promote mutual growth and trade and avoid conflicts between countries.

Avoid Conflict

Settle matters quickly with your adversary who is taking you to court. Do it while you are still together on the way, or your adversary may hand you over to the judge, and the judge may hand you over to the officer, and you may be thrown into prison. (Matt. 5:25)

When Jesus said to "settle matters quickly with your adversary," the idea was to avoid wars. When God instructed the people of Israel in the time of Moses, he established a law regarding war: "When you march up to attack a city, make its people an offer of peace" (Deut. 20:10). Armed conflict drains resources and should be the last resort. Jesus went one step further. He taught us to love our enemies.

The apostle Paul also gave us a beautiful lesson: "Do nothing out of selfish ambition or vain conceit. Rather, in humility value others above yourselves" (Phil. 2:3). This doesn't mean we forgo our authority or dignity, but we should avoid conflicts and presumptuousness. When we are at the top of a company or organization, we can impose authority without being aggressive.

People tend to value those who seek solutions for conflicts and are wary of those who arouse further trouble.

In his seventeenth-century classic *The Art of Worldly Wisdom*, Baltasar Gracián, one of the most important writers of the Spanish Baroque style, provides solid advice that is still followed today by strategists and politicians. The title of Gracián's last piece of advice is "In a Word: Be a Saint." He praises virtue as the connection to all perfection: "Three HHH's make a man happy: Health, Holiness, and a Headpiece. Virtue is the sun of the microcosm, and has for hemisphere a good conscience. She is so beautiful that she finds favour with both God and man. A man's capacity and greatness are to be measured by his virtue and not by his fortune."[1]

Gracián's advice, given more than three hundred years ago, has been in the Bible for almost two thousand years: "But just as he who called you is holy, so be holy in all you do" (1 Pet. 1:15). No one loses out by acting properly and earning the respect of others. Therefore, behave in such a manner that your friends and enemies can vouch for your dignity.

When you are recognized for your virtues, jealous people will often target you and try to destroy the good impression that you have created. At times like these, be patient, not responding to provocations, and let time do its job. Truth will usually win out. People's jealousy of you is a sign of your success—an uncomfortable sign, but a sign nonetheless.

Perhaps there are people in your life who do not treat you with the same respect and concern that you show them. That is human nature. It is not uncommon to give goodness and, in exchange, receive insults, slander, deception, or ingratitude.

The example of Jesus is an interesting one. The Bible reveals that some of the people he became involved with and even helped despised him. But this did not prevent his teachings from spreading farther afield. Turning his back on ingratitude, Jesus pursued his mission. That is what we have to do. Of the multitude of those we help and with whom we are honest, we will build an army of grateful, worthy people who will be at our side. This takes time and is worth its weight in gold, in both our personal and professional lives.

Therefore, do good, be cooperative, and strive for peace. Some people may attempt to take advantage of your good nature, but many others will want to associate with you and your good name. So keep calm; your friends will jump to your defense when needed. Remember that it is not when times are good that you discover who your true friends are but when times get tough: "A friend loves at all times, and a brother is born for a time of adversity" (Prov. 17:17).

Even difficult moments can be positive, then. In those moments you discover who your real friends are.

Keep a Positive Attitude

> And the Lord's servant must not be quarrelsome but must be kind to everyone, able to teach, not resentful. (2 Tim. 2:24)

The secret behind good relationships is discretion. Don't annoy your audience. Don't let people get sick of you; don't be that cloying individual. Leave before you are asked to do so. Don't force intimacy. Heed Solomon's warning: "Seldom set foot in your neighbor's house—too much of you, and they will hate you" (Prov. 25:17).

Avoid complimenting yourself at all costs. When at a meeting, get straight to the point, give your message, and graciously leave as soon as possible. As Rolim Amaro, pilot and founder of TAM airlines (now LATAM airlines), is attributed as saying, it is better to have someone that you have to pull back in than someone that you have to push out.

Eduardo Almeida, a corporate coach, affirms that in today's world, theoretical knowledge is not enough. You need professional skills, a good posture, and good relationships. At the Educar event in São Paulo in 2012, he brought our attention to the fact that in the corporate world 80 percent of all dismissals are due to attitude (behavior) and only 20 percent to technical failures (knowledge).[2]

The research called *Executives* performed by Catho regarding hiring, dismissal, and careers points out that 17.6 percent of layoffs are due to relationship issues (not getting along with coworkers and bosses and not being an effective supervisor), and 9.3 percent of layoffs can be attributed to excessive absences and delays. Five percent of employees are dismissed for lack of energy, 14.7 percent for lack of expertise, and 28 percent for poor performance.[3]

One of the most important qualities of people who want to thrive as part of a team is the ability to forgive and let go of mistakes and insults. It's important to not be overly sensitive and not hold grudges. Successful people don't take offense, don't speak harsh words, and don't retaliate. They have generous spirits with people who are weaker or difficult to handle. These are valuable characteristics.

Avoid participating in fights, disputes, and litigations. The best defense is not to harm. It is a simple solution that takes a lot of discipline. In the Bible, Solomon says, "It is to one's honor to avoid strife, but every fool is quick to quarrel" (Prov. 20:3), and, "A gentle answer turns away wrath, but a harsh word stirs up anger" (Prov. 15:1). When you choose peace instead of war you become a delightful person to be around, you walk a lighter road, and you keep the focus on productivity.

Solomon gives another important piece of advice: "A person's wisdom yields patience; it is to one's glory to overlook an offense" (Prov. 19:11). The biblical text has many different translations. In order to fully understand this advice, here are a few of them:

The discretion of a man deferreth his anger; and it is his glory to pass over a transgression. (KJV)

Experience makes you more patient, and you are most patient when you ignore insults. (ERV)

It's wise to be patient and show what you are like by forgiving others. (CEV)

A man's understanding makes him slow to anger. It is to his honor to forgive and forget a wrong done to him. (NLV)

If people would follow this advice, there would be less fighting. As the saying goes, "It takes two to tango."

Doesn't the Market Require You to Be Aggressive?

> Do not plot harm against your neighbor, who lives trustfully near you. Do not accuse anyone for no reason—when they have done you no harm. (Prov. 3:29–30)

When you choose to follow the path of pacifism and nonviolence according to the Law of Agreement, you will likely have at least one critic who will ask, "But doesn't the market require you to be aggressive?" Yes, it does, but this aggression is not directed toward individuals or companies. Your aggressive posture in the marketplace is related to your ability to innovate, to acquire clients, to give visibility to your product, and to offer the most efficient service at lower prices.

We want to overcome our competition, not destroy it. It is possible to be successful in the marketplace without harming others. The market is large and growing; there is room for everyone who follows the Law of Agreement.

Be like the sandalwood, which perfumes the ax that wounds it.
CHINESE PROVERB

18

The Law of Usefulness

> People who take care of fig trees are allowed to eat the
> fruit. In the same way, people who take care of their
> masters will be rewarded.
>
> Proverbs 27:18 ERV

The Bible considers it a sin when you can be useful but aren't or
can do good but don't. The biblical term *sin* does not refer only
to killing, lying, committing adultery, or stealing. In other words,
sin is not just about doing things that are wrong. Sin is also about
not doing the right things. Failing to do good is wrong: "If anyone,
then, knows the good they ought to do and doesn't do it, it is sin
for them" (James 4:17). The Bible urges people to be useful. You
can follow the Law of Usefulness either for religious reasons—to
avoid committing a sin—or simply because you want to be a successful professional.

There are many who think they don't need to serve others because they need no one. So they choose isolation, sometimes out of shyness or pride. But this behavior limits their professional development. Jesus was clear when he said: "Anyone who wants to be first must be the very last, and the servant of all" (Mark 9:35). In this context, being a "servant" is another way of saying you should be useful to everyone.

No company will hire you to fulfill your own needs. You are hired because of the company's needs. A company needs to be profitable to survive, otherwise it ends up in bankruptcy. In his parable of the bags of gold, Jesus dealt with an amazing principle regarding trust and professional career advancement. The employee who produced a return of 100 percent on his master's business received the following reward: "Well done, good and faithful servant! You have been faithful with a few things; I will put you in charge of many things. Come and share your Master's happiness" (Matt. 25:21).

How many employees want to be "faithful with a few things," hoping one day to be good and devoted managers of "many things"? Many expect to be promoted first and later to show their dedication to work. First you must prove yourself to be faithful over minor tasks.

Why would a manager promote someone who has not yet proven to be a good worker? Some people don't succeed because they fail to make a profit for the company. Some even put the company at risk with their poor management. Results will always reveal reality, and the negative outcomes for these employees are mere consequence.

But the well-prepared, honest, and committed professional who delivers results will be much sought after for the top jobs.

Sometimes auctions are held to determine who will hire the star player for their company by offering the best salary and benefits.

Do You Know What You Are Good At?

I'm not where I need to be, but thank God I'm not where I used to be. I'm OK, and I'm on my way.

Joyce Meyer

Discover how you can be most useful to the company. Learn what you are good at and focus on it. If you aren't yet good at anything, work hard at excelling in something. When an employee becomes more and more useful, there comes a time when he or she becomes essential.

It doesn't matter if the company is yours or someone else's, if it belongs to your family or a foreign group. It doesn't matter if your current job is good for your long-term career or not. If you are there, be useful to the company and to all those you deal with.

Solomon says, "Whoever protects their master will be honored" (Prov. 27:18b). A perceptive manager will treat employees well, reward their efforts, and keep them motivated and productive. But it may not always happen. Sometimes being treated with honor is an invitation to work elsewhere. If the company where you work fails to notice who deserves better treatment, sooner or later someone in another company will take notice.

If you are a manager, be alert to those deserving to be treated with honor and see to it. If you own the company, take notice of what the Bible recommends: "The one who guards a fig tree will eat its fruit" (Prov. 27:18a). This includes employees sharing in the company's profits and receiving their labor law entitlements.

If the company is doing well, its success should be good for everyone. By acting fairly and sharing the "fruit" of its profits with its employees, the company stands to gain a good reputation, not to mention the loyalty of its staff. This can only result in greater success. If things are currently not going well, try to adopt these recommendations; perhaps conditions will change for the better.

Win-Win

> One person gives freely, yet gains even more; another withholds unduly, but comes to poverty. (Prov. 11:24)

If someone makes too much at someone else's expense, he or she may lose it one day. However, what seems to be a loss for one may, in time, result in a gain.

If a deal is worthwhile for only some of the people involved, it won't last long and will likely cause some resentment. This can drive the injured party to seek a less exploitive relationship. Your goal should be to establish positive relationships in which everyone wins.

There are several types of relationships:

- Lose-Lose
- Win-Lose
- Lose-Win
- Win-Win

Only win-win relationships prevail over time and produce lasting alliances. Therefore, anyone who makes more than what is reasonable or fair does so at his or her own risk. Excessive profit is dangerous for business relationships. Perhaps someone thinks it is unwise not to make as much as possible, but if you analyze the situation carefully you will see that excessive earnings by one partner breed resentment in corporate and commercial partnerships.

In economics there is a graph known as the Laffer Curve, which shows that tax revenue is only progressive up to a certain level. When taxation becomes excessive, government revenues from taxes start to decline, whether because of evasion or lower economic activity within the tax generation base.[1]

We assert that the Laffer Curve can be applied to business. When someone exploits their business partners, alliances, customers, suppliers, managers, or employees, profit will rise to a certain point but then start to decline. And it will decline to lower levels than would have occurred if the individual had acted properly and honestly. The loss may arise from breaking up the business, a reduction in orders, or a lack of companionship and motivation.

We are not telling you to be a Goody Two-shoes, just to be good. And we are not telling you to be a wimp but to be honest. This is a truth everyone recognizes but few apply: everything you do will come back to you.

Today, we (the authors) are reaping many good things because we have been sowing them for twenty or thirty years. The earlier you sow, and the more you sow, the more you will reap. This is the Law of Sowing, which we will explore soon, and it will affect you in a positive way when you are useful to your neighbor and work with the win-win idea in mind.

Teamwork

They help each other and say to their companions, "Be strong!" (Isa. 41:6)

When you apply the Law of Usefulness—whether to a team or to the win-win concept—the ability to be a team player is very important. The image of the solitary scientist working alone and discovering a vaccine is a thing of the past. The majority of modern information and resources from various fields of knowledge and their interfaces resulted from teamwork. Nor can we imagine an efficient doctor or lawyer without a team, not to mention accountant or engineer. We all need help and relationships in order to produce more and better.

The business landscape is currently in dire need of groups or teams that can work in a harmonious manner. It is not by accident that most of the great names that we know of had to go into business with other people in order to achieve their objectives. They sought out people who followed their line of thought.

Napoleon Hill noted that the union of two or more minds generated a whole that was greater than the sum of its parts, which he called Master Mind.[2] On their own, none of them would have achieved the success they did. Only a team can create this kind of synergy.

In a lecture at the HSM Management Brazil Expo in 2010, Jim Collins, author of *Built to Last* and one of the world's most respected thinkers in the management field, pronounced that we have to build teams with the right people in the right positions. To do this he offers the following helpful tips. The right people:

- Identify with the company's core values;
- Don't need close supervision/micromanagement (they are self-motivated and responsible);
- Understand that they don't have a job, but rather responsibilities;

- Do what they have agreed to do, keep their word;
- Are mature in front of the mirror and the window;
- Are able to grow with their position and responsibilities;
- Have enormous passion for the company and for what they do.

The fifth item, regarding the "mirror" and the "window," is worth explaining. A poor professional, when everything is going well, looks in the mirror and attributes his success to himself. When things go wrong, he looks out the window, trying to put the blame on others. A good professional and team worker does the opposite: when things are going well, he attributes the success to the team (he goes to the window); when things go wrong, he asks himself what he could have done to avoid the problem (he looks in the mirror).

You won't be successful for long by kicking those around you.
LEE IACOCCA

19

The Law of Advice

Plans fail for lack of counsel; but with many advisers
they succeed.

PROVERBS 15:22

The Law of Advice states that before you make an important decision you should seek counsel from several advisers, preferably with
varied backgrounds and outlooks on the world. It recommends
getting a second opinion and, if you can, a third. You will make
the final decision, but only after listening to a good many wise
people or after reading a reasonable amount of material about the
matter in question.

There are those who seek advice from only one person or read
just one book and as a result have only one way of seeing things.
That's not the most effective way of coming to a decision. The
Japanese have a saying, "No matter how small a stone is, nobody
can see all of its sides at the same time." Gandhi said that every truth

has seven points of view, all of which are correct by themselves but not correct at the same time and in the same circumstances.

Having only a single adviser is risky, even if that person is your guru, boss, superior, mentor, coach, pastor, priest, parent, or whoever. Making mistakes is human, which is why it is good to have many advisers, even if you give greater consideration to one over the other. Having just one person deciding everything in your life is to raise that person to a divine status, and the Ten Commandments warn us about the danger of assigning this status to a person (Exod. 20:3). And if you don't believe in God, that's just one more reason not to hand this burden to another human being.

Having multiple advisers is also recommended in the book of Proverbs: "The wise prevail through great power, and those who have knowledge muster their strength. Surely you need guidance to wage war, and victory is won through many advisers" (24:5–6). Learn by asking those who know more than you.

When you listen to someone, analyze his or her past experience and carefully evaluate whether the person is acting in good faith or out of purely personal interest, so that there is no conflict of interest between you. Your favorite adviser may not have the proper advice to give you. Dialectics are always important for creating sound, well-argued opinions. Therefore, whenever you can, listen to different opinions or versions of the story.

Feedback

As iron sharpens iron, so one person sharpens another. (Prov. 27:17)

When Solomon talks about two kinds of sharpening in Proverbs 27:17, he is referring to both teaching and feedback, which is similar to advice. Asking for and considering feedback is a step toward excellence, a way of developing competence.

Feedback in communication is the "information the issuer obtains from the receiver's reaction to his message and which serves to evaluate the results of the transmission."[1] In electricity and electronics, feedback is frequency return. In our day-to-day lives, it is the ability to give and receive opinions, criticism, and suggestions regarding what to do.

In order to know if we are on the right path, we need feedback from others. Companies launch new products and services based on consumers' feedback. Customer service gathers feedback to make sure the company is doing a good job, and companies use feedback to improve the performance of managers and employees. Feedback can also be the starting point for important changes in a marriage and in relationships in general.

According to Raul Candeloro, "In school they don't teach us to give and receive feedback. We learn the hard way: with the scars from our failure to plan and the unexpected responses that life throws in our face. The interesting thing is that we know how to criticize, but giving feedback is more than that. We need to know how to do this properly if we are to actually change something in a constructive manner."[2]

No leader or entrepreneur will get very far without intensely developing his or her ability to give and receive feedback. "A company where everyone is gagged might even be profitable in the short term, but it will certainly be a toxic environment to work in and will have to change to grow in the long term," adds Candeloro.[3]

In his book, *Qual é o Tamanho dos Seus Sonhos?* (*How great are your dreams?*), Ebenézer Bittencourt lists several important tips about the advantages and skills involved in feedback.

Advantages to receiving feedback:

- It enhances the commitment of subordinates.
- It determines whether the message was heard, understood, and accepted.
- It makes people feel recognized and appreciated and willing to follow the leader.

Skills involved in giving feedback:

- Describe behavior instead of evaluating people.
- Be specific, don't generalize.
- Focus on behavior that can be changed.
- Speak on your behalf, not "on behalf of the group."
- Accept responsibility for your acts, perceptions, and feelings.
- Be certain that the feedback you give will help rather than punish the receiver.
- Give more positive than negative feedback.
- Verify the clarity and precision of what was understood.[4]

In *Principles of Leadership*, Ken Blanchard says the following: "I firmly believe that feedback is the most profitable strategy for improving performance and inducing satisfaction. It doesn't take long, it's free and it can make employees change quickly."[5]

When was the last time you received or asked people for feedback about your work, your performance, or the products or services you sell? What about how you are doing as a parent, spouse, child, or friend? You can use these responses to evaluate and improve your performance or relationship.

When you receive positive feedback, be grateful—but don't get carried away with the compliments. The better you are, the more cautious you need to be so as not to become a victim of success—thinking that you are so good that you can do no wrong.

When you receive negative feedback, be thankful as well and check to what extent the criticism is valid. Always look at feedback as an expert report, capable of enabling you to analyze problems and resolve them before things get worse. Feedback is an instrument, a tool, and a path to your personal growth.

There are several sources of feedback: friends, coworkers, the job market, and enemies or competitors.

The first and best is the feedback we get from our friends. Friends who are sincere and tell the truth help us to improve. There are people who are mere apple polishers, unwilling to correct, criticize, and disagree with anyone. Their opinions are worthless. A good friend is one who accepts you and loves you, but who will also point out to you where you can improve. Solomon says, "Wounds from a friend can be trusted, but an enemy multiplies kisses" (Prov. 27:6).

The second type of feedback comes from people who, even if they aren't our friends, are willing to give their opinion—such as a coworker. This feedback is especially valuable because it may relate to the work environment or best practices.

The third type of feedback is the one we get from the job market. This feedback comes through studying statistics, reading research, or analyzing surveys and questionnaires.

Another source of feedback is our enemies or competitors. We shouldn't use what they say as a guide to our actions, but however spiteful their criticisms and comments may be, they can be a source of valuable information. Perhaps your friends and customers, out of consideration for you, don't mention your flaws. But your enemy won't hesitate to point out your weaknesses. Most of your enemies will criticize you behind your back, but if their criticism makes it to your ears, check whether their insights are valid and, if so, make the most of the opportunity to correct your actions.

It takes courage and discipline to ask people for their opinions and to allow them to critique you freely. It takes humility and maturity to resist being offended when someone contradicts you. And it takes determination and strength to overcome your resistance to change when needed.

Be careful when giving feedback or advising someone else. Be concise and cautious with your suggestions, advice, or criticisms. Don't try to advise someone regarding something you know nothing about. Only do it if absolutely necessary or if someone asks you to. Some people ask for advice, but deep down they don't want to hear the truth. If you give advice to a wise person he or she will thank you, but an ignorant person will become irritated with you. Solomon's advice: "Do not rebuke mockers or they will hate you; rebuke the wise and they will love you" (Prov. 9:8).

Feedback is the breakfast of champions.
RICK TATE

20

The Law of Leadership

[Those] who direct the affairs of the church well are
worthy of double honor.

1 TIMOTHY 5:17

No one advances in life without some degree of leadership. You
may not want to lead others, but you will not be successful if you
don't learn to be at least your own leader. And if you learn to be your
own leader, leading others will come naturally. Make the decision
to apply the Law of Leadership to your life. Be the boss of your own
actions and lead yourself down the path of success. Do this and
other people will be inspired by you and will eventually follow you.

Carlos Wizard Martins, founder of the Wizard language teaching
method and owner of one of the world's three largest companies
in this field, offers several leadership tips in his book *Desperte o
Milionário que Há em Você* (roughly translated as *Awake the millionaire within you*), of which we have selected three:

- Create solutions, not problems.
- Focus on people, not on structures.
- Love what you do.[1]

Martins also advises that you not try to change others. Instead, change yourself.[2] This is the road map not only to success but also to becoming a leader. After all, as Gandhi taught us, those who cannot govern themselves will not be capable of governing others.

Leadership is achieved based on the trust you create, and trust is built on three pillars: character, competence, and communication. These pillars are essential to being a good leader. And following the Golden Rule will make you a natural leader. People follow those who treat them with care and respect. Sun Tzu, one of the greatest strategists of all time, taught: "Protect your soldiers as you would protect a newborn and they will follow you into the deepest valleys; care for your soldiers as you would for your dearest children, and they will readily meet death under your command."[3] The manner in which you treat others will inspire your team and your customers.

Several attitudes can help to improve the quality of your professional and leadership skills. We can learn much from applying the truths we read in Paul's Letter to the Romans:

> If [your gift] is serving, then serve; if it is teaching, then teach; if it is to encourage, then give encouragement; if it is giving, then give generously; if it is to lead, do it diligently; if it is to show mercy, do it cheerfully.
>
> Love must be sincere. Hate what is evil; cling to what is good. Be devoted to one another in love. Honor one another above yourselves. Never be lacking in zeal, but keep your spiritual fervor, serving the Lord. Be joyful in hope, patient in affliction, faithful

in prayer. Share with the Lord's people who are in need. Practice hospitality.

Bless those who persecute you; bless and do not curse. Rejoice with those who rejoice; mourn with those who mourn. Live in harmony with one another. Do not be proud, but be willing to associate with people of low position. Do not be conceited.

Do not repay anyone evil for evil. Be careful to do what is right in the eyes of everyone. If it is possible, as far as it depends on you, live at peace with everyone. Do not take revenge, my dear friends, but leave room for God's wrath, for it is written: "It is mine to avenge; I will repay," says the Lord. On the contrary:

> "If your enemy is hungry, feed him;
>   if he is thirsty, give him something to drink.
> In doing this, you will heap burning coals on his head."

Do not be overcome by evil, but overcome evil with good. (Rom. 12:7–21)

Authority

Do not be bosses over the people you lead. Live as you would like to have them live. (1 Pet. 5:13 NLV)

Professionals, employees, and self-employed professionals must know how to deal with authority in order to climb the ladder of success. There will always be people above and below us, and knowing how to handle both situations correctly is a must.

We recommend that bosses and supervisors behave professionally and in such a manner as to make their authority natural and unquestioned. It is important that their employees obey and respect their orders both from the technical point of view and as a matter of trust. The words of the king in Antoine de Saint Exupéry's classic *The Little Prince* come to mind: "Accepted authority rests first of all on reason."[4] Or, as J. Oswald Sanders says: "True greatness, true leadership, is found in giving yourself in service to others, not in coaxing or inducing others to serve you."[5] Those in the position of employee or service provider must take other precautions. Be pleasant and respectful, but not in the sense of flattery, and serve well.

Being a pleasant and dedicated professional is easy when things are going well. But the Bible knows the workings of the mind and emotions of all and instructs us that even in difficult situations, we must see to it that loyalty and respect for others prevail, whether they are right or not:

> Slaves, in reverent fear of God submit yourselves to your masters, not only to those who are good and considerate, but also to those who are harsh. (1 Pet. 2:18)

> Teach slaves to be subject to their masters in everything, to try to please them, not to talk back to them, and not to steal from them, but to show that they can be fully trusted. (Titus 2:9–10)

Showing respect for hierarchy at work goes beyond the normal duty of an employee. Respect for authority is a rare virtue in the era of individualism and relativism in which we live. For Christians, though, respect for authority is based on our relationship with and dependence on God.

By its very nature a professional relationship allows a person to resign and leave a difficult situation. That is why bad bosses lose good employees. There is nothing worse than an arrogant boss who thinks he can do whatever he wants. Similarly, an employee who disrespects his supervisors will be treated negatively by the market. So, when we talk about respecting authority we see three basic notions:

1. The choice to quit a job or company, if you wish;
2. The responsibility on the part of employees to respect authority;
3. The responsibility on the part of employers and managers to make proper use of the authority they enjoy.

All of us know an overbearing boss who is never satisfied and has unreasonable demands. And we all know an employee with a "bare minimum" attitude toward work who cannot deal with pressure or demands of any kind and who constantly thinks he or she is being exploited. These are extreme cases that require patience, tolerance, and resilience.

If, when all is said and done, you discover that you just cannot work with a specific person, finish your tasks or fulfill your end of the agreement and then choose not to work with that person in the future. If the pressure or discomfort reaches an unreasonable level, look for a coach, mentor, or more experienced friend to assess the situation and help you deal with it. If needed, use the law; it's there to protect everyone, including you.

True leadership cannot be awarded, appointed, or assigned. It comes only from influence, and that cannot be mandated. It must be earned.
JOHN MAXWELL

PART 5

Laws concerning Personal Growth

21

The Law of Gratitude

Evil will never leave the house of one who pays back
evil for good.

PROVERBS 17:13

Do you know the difference between a human being and a dog? If
you find a sick, abandoned, and hungry dog on the street and you
give it food, shelter, medication, and love, he will never bite you.
As for the human . . .

This story is a great illustration of human behavior. Gratitude
has become a rare virtue. Either gratitude is nonexistent or it easily fades away. Very few people have it in them to be thankful and
remain loyal to those who have helped them. When Jesus cured ten
lepers, only one of them came back to thank him (Luke 17:11–19).
Ten percent. That's how it is with human beings.

There are two lessons here. First, when people are ungrateful, put
your heart at ease, because that is the norm. Second, don't become
yet another ungrateful person on the face of the earth.

This is the Law of Gratitude: don't bite the hand that feeds you. Keep your promises, and if at any time this is no longer possible, behave in a straightforward manner, sit down with whomever you have a bone to pick, and resolve it in the most positive way possible.

Bad-mouthing others, getting involved in unfair or illegal actions, participating in corporate espionage, or deliberately doing something to jeopardize your coworkers and supervisors are improper attitudes and actions. Besides the moral damage, these choices also put your reputation and image at risk.

A good way to conduct job interviews is to allow the candidate to speak freely about his professional experiences. Job applicants who criticize their former bosses can be dismissed immediately. After all, if an interviewee is quick to criticize his former employer, why would he act any differently with a new one?

Gratitude has to be renewed constantly. Don't take help for granted, and don't forget those who have lent you a helping hand in the past. Many do, but try to be different; become an above-average professional.

When put into practice, gratitude begins by thanking those who deserve it. If we take it one step further, it will lead us to another law, that of generosity.

As we express our gratitude, we must never forget that the highest appreciation is not to utter words but to live by them.
JOHN F. KENNEDY

22

The Law of Generosity

A generous person will prosper; whoever refreshes
others will be refreshed.

PROVERBS 11:25

The Bible recommends that we be generous, in a joyful and unselfish manner. The Law of Generosity speaks to this type of attitude in two ways. First, you should not be attached to what you have. Second, you should not concern yourself with what others have. A generous person is willing to graciously give to others when someone is in need.

Andrew Carnegie, the king of steel of the twentieth century and the richest man of his time, was the first businessman to publicly state that the wealthy had the moral obligation to share their fortunes. He helped to build 2,800 schools, libraries, museums, and other educational institutions. In 1901 he sold his company for over $480 million. By his death in 1919, he had donated over

$350 million. The saying "The man who dies rich, dies disgraced" is attributed to him.[1] Steve Jobs reportedly said that there would be no purpose in "being the richest man in the graveyard." Warren Buffett and Bill Gates together built the Giving Pledge, a commitment that billionaires make to give half of their fortunes to charity.[2] To date, more than one hundred billionaires have accepted this commitment, including Larry Ellison, the founder of Oracle; film director George Lucas; and Mark Zuckerberg and Priscilla Chan of Facebook. Don't wait until you become a billionaire to begin to give generously.

Some people refuse to donate to others because they fear they are being exploited. Others do not donate because they think those receiving the donation are somehow taking advantage of their generosity, either because they are lazy or otherwise unworthy. Still others do not give because they are selfish or overly attached to their money. Some people donate but out of vanity, not generosity, to receive the benefits of being socially admired or simply to feel good about themselves.

Jesus spoke of helping others as a political strategy. A rich man was told his manager was taking advantage of his fortune (see Luke 16). He then asked the manager, "What is this I hear about you? Give an account of your management, because you cannot be manager any longer" (v. 2). Terrified of losing his job, the manager had an idea to earn the gratitude of others that one day would work on his behalf. So he called his boss's debtors. "How much do you owe my master?" he asked the first one. "Nine hundred gallons of olive oil," the man replied. And the manager told him, "Take your bill . . . and make it four hundred and fifty" (vv. 5–6). And so he did to all the debtors.

Despite the manager's improper attitude, his master noticed this clever move and praised him for it: "The master commended the dishonest manager because he had acted shrewdly" (v. 8). The manager was about to be fired, and the rich man recognized the manager's generosity as his strategy for building his good name in the market.

When you can, help those around you, but not for ulterior motives and certainly not with other people's money. Remember that generosity is productive, and your actions will be registered in the hearts and minds of those you help.

The Law of Generosity has worked for William on many occasions, as in the story that follows:

> I wanted to buy a piece of property, but when I contacted the owner, he said he was about to close the deal with another buyer. However, a few days later he called to tell me the property was mine if I still wanted it. As we were signing the deed he told me that at the first opportunity he had, he pulled out of the deal with the other potential buyer to give me priority. And what was the reason?
>
> Years earlier, his wife had worked for me on a prep course. She became ill, and although she wasn't able to teach the classes, I continued sending her a paycheck. It wasn't my obligation because our agreement was to pay only if teachers showed up to teach. But I paid anyway. The money came in handy, not just for daily expenses but for the medication she needed. Many years had gone by since then and his wife had died, but my generosity wasn't forgotten. This generosity was what granted me the deal.

Solomon puts it this way: "Ship your grain across the sea; after many days you may receive a return" (Eccles. 11:1). William did have ulterior motives: he did what he thought was the right thing to do and what he would want to happen if he were in the same situation—acting according to the Law of Love. He just shipped his grains across the sea, and some time later he received his return, multiplied back to him.

You can never predict how you will be rewarded for the good you do, but rest assured, you will be rewarded somehow.

In order to put the Law of Generosity into practice, learn not to become overly attached to things or money and to believe that the more you do with your life, the greater the returns. We know of dozens of cases when someone helped others when he or she was doing well, and later, in the midst of a personal or market crisis, the acts of kindness were remembered and the favors returned.

Social Marketing

> Don't be interested only in your own life, but care about the lives of others too. (Phil. 2:4 ERV)

The Bible recommends showing solidarity with and social responsibility to our neighbors. Many companies prefer to negotiate with companies and to hire people who are generous and socially conscious. Generosity should be the result of altruism, but there are companies that use what is called "social marketing" to try to improve their image in society.

The person receiving help doesn't care about the internal motivation of the person or company helping them. The recipient only knows that his or her hunger and cold are diminished.

At a higher level, from a human (not necessarily religious) perspective, we desire generous people to give not simply to be seen and to do more than just give alms and old clothes, although these certainly can be very useful. Ideally one should, as has been said, teach one to fish rather than merely give a fish.

We strongly believe in social work focused not just on immediate needs but on redeeming people from situations of need and poverty. Assistance programs, both private and governmental, should provide an exit door from poverty. Education and vocational training are good ways of giving people back their dignity.

Social Responsibility

> Be true to your servant for good; let not the proud ones oppress me. (Ps. 119:122)

When we talk about the Law of Generosity, we are not just talking about helping the poor or being there for our coworkers. Social responsibility includes other factors such as profit sharing, how profits are used, environmental liability, respect for universal values, and others.

Although they are still a minority, some successful professionals are concerned with these issues. An article published in the Brazilian magazine *Exame* raised an interesting discussion about how the population and the corporate world perceive profits. Here is an excerpt: "In general, the Brazilian population does not agree that profit should be the paramount objective of a company. When interviewed by the Brazilian opinion research company Instituto Vox Populi, 93% of Brazilians felt that creating jobs was the mission of private enterprise, contradicting the opinion of 82% of company CEOs, who put profit first."[3] Nevertheless, there are companies that don't see profits as the end all and be all, as is the case with the beauty company Natura, whose mission is "to create value for society," according to their website.[4]

Hence, according to the Law of Generosity, you should concern yourself with these concepts and universal values: respect the laws, people's health, and the environment; share your profits; and choose some kind of social program to engage in.

Where social projects are concerned, we believe it is incumbent on the government to provide assistance to those in need. However, there is nothing preventing companies and individuals from taking an active interest in such projects, especially because the benefits of doing good also fall on those who practice it.

Profit Sharing

All day long he craves for more, but the righteous give without sparing. (Prov. 21:26)

Companies today have a variety of systems that offer rewards, motivation, and commissions, which is a positive thing. The idea is that at the end of a monthly, semiannual, or annual period, companies distribute part of their earnings to their employees. This is not only a motivating factor but also a way of distributing income, making people rich, and boosting the economy.

As we discussed in the chapter on the Law of Usefulness, the Bible says, "People who take care of fig trees are allowed to eat the fruit. In the same way, people who take care of their masters will be rewarded" (Prov. 27:18 ERV). If your employee helped to look after the "fig tree" and had the company's well-being at heart, then it is only fair that he be rewarded with a share of the fruit. And he should receive not only a salary and benefits but also something more, whether in the form of profit sharing, paid education, breaks, trips, and so on.

True generosity is an offering; given freely and out of pure love. No strings attached. No expectations.

SUZE ORMAN

23

The Law of Contentment

But if we have food and clothing, we will be content
with that.

1 TIMOTHY 6:8

If you are content where you are, the Law of Contentment will
afford you the patience and serenity to grow, if you wish. If you
are not content, this law can show you how to be fulfilled with
what you already have. There are those who are content being an
attorney, for example, but due to pressure from their parents or
society, they built their careers and became court judges instead.
These people will likely become frustrated.

In his book *Clássicos do Mundo Corporativo* (*Classic stories from
the corporate world*), Max Gehringer, a Brazilian career coach, describes the principles behind the Law of Contentment by sharing
a story about a man named Valdemar.

I once worked at a company with a salesman called Valdemar. Valdemar enjoyed being a salesman so much that when anyone asked him his name he would answer: "Valdemar, with a V for vendor."

Valdemar was so good at his job that one day we decided to promote him to supervisor. We called Valdemar to announce his new promotion, expecting him to jump out of the chair, hug everyone and burst into tears of joy. Contrary to our expectations, he simply answered:

"I am extremely grateful, but no, thank you."

Valdemar's supervisor could hardly contain his disbelief.

"How come, Valdemar? We offer you a chance like this and you turn it down? Don't you have ambition?"

To which Valdemar replied: "Of course I do. Lots of it. My ambition is to be the best salesman in the company."[1]

Gehringer says that Valdemar continued in his job for many years, as happy as the day is long. All the executives kept asking themselves how many "Valdemars" there were in the company— people who were content with what they were doing, who didn't feel like giving up half an hour with their family at the end of the day in exchange for a 10 percent salary increase and longer working hours. These were people who didn't wish to be promoted, contrary to what ambitious managers and directors thought. "At the end of the day, it is the 'Valdemars' that sustain a business. Directors come and go, but the 'Valdemars' remain. They don't want more money; they want more respect. In businesses, there is a day for everything, but every day is Valdemar's day," Gehringer concludes.[2]

Companies need people like that. It's interesting to note how quite often we see people who are looking for a promotion, and when they get it they don't do as well in their new position. The ideal is that everyone does what they do best. And the way we see it, Valdemar is, in fact, a successful person.

As a rule, society defines people as successful when they have money, fame, influence, and many people working for them. But this view has been questioned by those who believe in more refined concepts, who define success as being well with oneself, being happy, enjoying respect in one's community.[3] Quite often this can be much more important than fame and power. Which is more important for you: personal achievement based on your own criteria or ready-made forms of success?

In this globalized world, success is often viewed as getting a university degree, having a brand-new car, buying your own home, and becoming the president of a company. Success is generally seen as making it to the top. But as we have already mentioned, in the Bible and in a wiser and more sophisticated view of life, success is being where you are, who you are, and content with your lot. It's the way you walk, not where you are heading. Success is, above all, a trajectory in which a person, regardless of where he or she is, continues to advance, or at least does not retreat. And we are not only talking about financially measurable attributes.

Your life, for example, may be a success today according to your evaluation. But many people will not consider it successful until you make a lot of money or appear in some glossy magazine. The world sees external realities; those who are more observant see your inner self. These externals may satisfy an imagination, but they don't always result in real benefits for you. On this subject Solomon said, "There is a way that appears to be right, but in the end it leads to death" (Prov. 16:25).

What ruler do you use to measure success?

If you are well balanced and aware of what you want, where you are, and where you are going, then you will be capable of studying, working, looking after your health and your relationships, and being an all-around successful person.

If you are the type who runs around like crazy in search of more and more money and success, you may need, as Laurence Peter says, "to be satisfied with stopping." He goes on: "In a society based on permanent ascension, learning to stop and finding peace is becoming difficult. In a world where quantity, wealth and power are worth more than quality and self-achievement, people tend to confuse ascension with satisfaction."[4]

Sometimes happiness and achievement mean rising a little higher in your career or investing a little more money. But quite often being smart means slowing your pace. We believe it takes enormous effort and dedication to rise in the world and to remain up-to-date. At the same time, we believe that growth should be something natural, built on solid and self-sustaining foundations. For example, we need to take good care of our families and protect our leisure time, not to mention our health, because as the years go by we become more susceptible to illnesses.

Growing indefinitely may not be a wise move, as we see in the entertaining story of Otto M. E. Canic, a competent employee of the We-Fix Workshop. Otto was satisfied with his job because it didn't involve paperwork and writing. One day his boss offered him a promotion to a managerial position. He wanted to turn down the offer, but his wife, Winnie, an active member of the League for the Social Enhancement of Women, insisted that he accept it. With a higher salary, the family's economic and social status would rise. Otto didn't want to do it but let himself be carried away by his wife's insistence and took the offer. Six months later, he's just been diagnosed with an ulcer. His marriage has hit the rocks as his wife accused him of having an affair with his new secretary, which led to her being fired as president of the League. He spends long hours in a job that leaves him frustrated and arrives home extremely irritated.

Another very competent mechanic and Otto's coworker, Niceguy, was also offered a promotion. But his wife, Sally, knowing how much he loved his work, told him to pass on the offer. Result? He continued to be the smiling and popular man he had been. Considered a youth leader and a dedicated worker, his bosses soon noticed his value to the company and rewarded him with a huge bonus, an advantageous contract, and a salary increase. The Niceguys live a comfortable and satisfactory existence.

The tale of these two men is useful. Here we see how the Law of Contentment works. You should never be desperate for growth, especially when you are already in a comfortable situation. The ability to be satisfied is an antidote to becoming a victim or a slave of your own success.

Whoever loves money never has enough; whoever loves wealth is never satisfied with their income. This too is meaningless.
ECCLESIASTES 5:10

24

The Law of Employability

Many claim to have unfailing love, but a faithful person
who can find?

PROVERBS 20:6

So far in this book you have gotten to know several biblical laws
that bring success. When you follow their guidance, you will be
obeying the Law of Employability. This is a system of behavior
whose hallmark is balance. The texts in the Bible are intimately
linked and this law, at the end of the day, is a review of the attitudes
and behaviors defended by the laws already mentioned. It can also
be called the Law of Aggregation.

Success is the result of a combination of recognizably valuable
attributes that are universally applicable, no matter your job or
position. And it is not by mistake that those attributes and characteristics are strongly recommended in the Bible.

163

The labor market is always in search of those who are

Hard workers	Determined and persistent
Competent	Patient
Honest	Humble
Pleasant	Team players
Loyal and reliable	Resilient

The first three qualities on the list are essential. In order to be a good business partner, life partner, boss, employee, or freelancer, you need all three of these—hard work, competence, and honesty. Warren Buffett mentions these first three characteristics using, respectively, the terms "energy," "intelligence," and "integrity":

energy = working hard (being devoted to one's work)

intelligence = competence, knowledge, skills (being competent)

integrity = honesty (being honest)[1]

One detail that shouldn't escape our attention is that the three qualities have to coexist. There's no use in a professional who is

- honest, but lazy or incompetent;
- a hard worker, but incompetent or dishonest; or
- competent, but lazy or dishonest.

If you combine honesty, competence, and hard work, then you are guaranteed to have a job—and if you lose this job, you will easily replace it. If your career is not on the right track, think about what changes you need to make to set things right.

The other seven attributes are important, but, depending on the circumstances, the absence of one of them may not be an issue.

Depending on your job, one or another may be more or less important. They will all, however, help to build a top professional.

Anyone with the three essential qualities and a good mix of the other seven will be ripe for job offers, partnerships, or investments. Success is a consequence, not a goal; it happens because the market values and demands these characteristics, no matter to what profession they are applied. Another highly valued attribute is leadership. But a person who has a good combination of the ten characteristics discussed tends to be a natural leader.

As we said earlier, a company won't hire you because of your needs but because of its needs. Therefore you must be indispensable to the company. People become indispensable as a result of some personal attribute or a combination of factors that can be achieved with study, training, and integrity.

In any case, what makes the most difference is the whole, the sum of your attributes. Have you noticed how some people who are not good looking are still considered attractive or become popular? That is due to the combination of their characteristics. Many film directors who have never won an Oscar win the Academy Award for lifetime achievement based on the sum of their work. Generally speaking, a single characteristic, however spectacular, won't guarantee success. You need a number of secondary attributes to make a statement, even if you do not excel at them.

Every human being has qualities and flaws, but we will be loved or hated depending on the sum of our parts. That's why the important thing is to have an overall positive combination of attributes. Some people focus on working on their weaknesses, while others focus on enhancing their strengths. Whatever your strategy, take care of the whole person. It's not easy, but the rewards are many and long lasting.

Combination of Management Practices

> Live a life worthy of the calling you have received. Be completely humble and gentle; be patient, bearing with one another in love. (Eph. 4:1–2)

The Law of Employability suggests you should have a wide range of qualities—a combination of virtues and principles that will enhance your career opportunities. The Law of Employability can also be applied to managing a business. Every entrepreneur or manager can evaluate his business using the Bible as a compass that validates his plans and actions. The Bible has a multidiscipline approach and, although it is not organized systematically (because that is not the purpose of Scripture), it brings clarity regarding a number of good practices.

The Bible doesn't use today's professional terminology, but it addresses modern concepts such as stop-loss, an investing concept on interrupting losses: "Watch out that you do not lose what [you] have worked for, but that you may be rewarded fully" (2 John 1:8). The concept of cash flow is mentioned in Luke 14:28: "Suppose one of you wants to build a tower. Won't you first sit down and estimate the cost to see if you have enough money to complete it?" These are just a couple of examples. If you want to study further, analyze the passages listed below:

Planning	
Logistics/finance	Joshua 1:11; Luke 14:28–32
Legal issues	Luke 20:25; Romans 13:3
Environmental issues	Genesis 1:28; Proverbs 12:10; Ecclesiastes 3:18
Investment, innovation, creativity	2 Chronicles 26:15
Excellence	Proverbs 22:29
Stop-loss	2 John 1:8

Managing People	
Developing your skills	Ephesians 4:1–2
Valuing your activities	1 Corinthians 12:20–21
Merit	Revelation 3:21
Leadership	Proverbs 28:1–4
Do they understand what to do?	Acts 8:30
Communication/connectivity	John 15:4
Do not harm your neighbor/ solidarity	1 Samuel 25:7; Ecclesiastes 11:2
Generosity	Ecclesiastes 11:1–2; Matthew 10:8
Personal Management	
Vision and communication of vision	Habakkuk 2:2; Acts 8:30
Self-care	1 Timothy 4:16
Humbleness	Proverbs 29:23
Respect authority	Romans 13:1–5
Excellence	Proverbs 9:10
Passion	Ecclesiastes 9:10
Discipline	Proverbs 5:23; 6:23; 23:23
Accept warnings	Proverbs 9:8; 10:17; 12:1; 15:5, 32; 17:10; 27:5; 29:11
Perseverance	Ecclesiastes 10:10
Management Values	
Ethics and transparency	Joshua 7:19; John 7:4
Sharing results	Proverbs 27:18; Acts 2:45
Willing to invest	Ecclesiastes 11:1; James 4:13

Luck

Casting the lot settles disputes and keeps strong opponents apart. (Prov. 18:18)

Solomon mentions luck in the proverb that opens this section. This reminds us that, sometimes, when competitors (such as athletes, teams, or companies) have a similar skill level, luck can be what tips the scale. In any kind of scenario, what we can do is be prepared, do our best, and see what happens.

If we win, we can celebrate our victory and honor our opponents. If we lose, we can try to be even more prepared next time. And, after we have done our part, we can hope for luck to shine on us.

Action speaks louder than words.
ABRAHAM LINCOLN

25

The Law of Sowing

A man reaps what he sows.

GALATIANS 6:7

We end our list of biblical laws with the Law of Sowing because, just like the Law of Employability, this law is a good way of summarizing all the biblical laws that we have covered. The Law of Employability boils down to personal qualities, and the Law of Sowing encompasses the logic of how success works.

Everyone recognizes that, generally speaking, the right attitudes create positive effects, while wrong or bad attitudes create negative effects. When you observe reality you see this played out. As a rule, working leads to benefits while sneakiness leads to problems. And so on.

The fact that religions recommend correct attitudes may lead people to assume that proper conduct is strictly a religious issue. It isn't. Religions may talk about heaven, hell, redemption, and so on, but that isn't our objective in this book. Our focus is success, and from the intellectual and logical point of view, positive results are not the privilege of only those who have faith but also those who abide by the values that lead to success. From a practical point of view, an atheist who obeys the biblical laws of success will enjoy much more professional respect than a religious person who doesn't obey these laws. The laws of success do not discriminate.

The Law of Sowing, also called the Law of Cause and Effect, states: we reap what we sow. This law of success says that everything you do comes back to you. All sources of human knowledge say this, including religion, philosophy, chemistry and biology, traditional physics (Newton's law), even quantum physics. They cannot all be wrong. At the end of the day, what you do comes back to you like a boomerang.

In fact, what you do will come back many times over. Life works like a boomerang, but one with multiplication powers. When you plant a single seed of a fruit, you will reap much fruit in the future; if you let a virus in, it will multiply into millions.

You are at liberty to sow or not to sow, and you can choose what to sow, but you are a slave to your choices. You will reap what you sow, at least until the day you decide to start planting other types of seeds.

Many religions look on this as a negative principle: "Do not do to others what you wouldn't like them to do to you." This is a good start, because what you do to others will come back to you one day. If you don't do evil, it won't come back to you. As we discussed earlier, Jesus took this principle into the positive field of assertiveness and action in his Golden Rule, which says you should do to others that which you desire to be done to you (Matt. 7:12).

Don't just stand there stagnating, waiting for things to happen. Start the ball rolling right away! That is how the Law of Sowing becomes active, proactive, and a creator of change. Treat your neighbors as well as you would like them to treat you. If that is your intent, you certainly won't gossip about them, take advantage of them, delay paying them a debt owed, or swindle them in some transaction. If you exploit your neighbor in any way, then you will pay for this behavior down the road.

Madeleine L'Engle wrote, "Love isn't how you feel. It's what you do."[1] Do good, and by it you will be loving your neighbor, whether a relative, friend, business partner, or consumer. The Law of Sowing combined with the Law of Love is an irresistible force.

The Bible says, "A faithful person will be richly blessed" (Prov. 28:20). This is true both in the religious sense and on the secular plane. A "faithful person" may be one who is faithful to God, but whoever is faithful to his employer will also be rewarded, as well as someone who is faithful to a client or to the quality of a product or service. There is more than one dimension to these biblical concepts—they have multiple applications.

Let's look at another example: If you are a faithful spouse, will you be rewarded? Regardless of any other benefit to your faithfulness, at least you will not have to deal with the pressures of secret relationships or being caught in the act of adultery. Even the airlines reward those who are faithful to them. Your fidelity is appreciated and rewarded with prizes. Imagine the rewards for fidelity in the important things of life!

A single biblical text can often be applied in many ways. What is certain here is that someone who is faithful (to someone or something) will be richly rewarded.

The Law of Sowing applies to every area of life. Everything you do will come back multiplied many times over. Therefore, do good deeds. Be wise, work hard, stay honest, and love your neighbor—and your professional life will be a success.

When the Law of Sowing Doesn't Work

Time and chance happen to them all. (Eccles. 9:11)

Some people question the applicability of the Law of Sowing, alleging that there are those who sow and don't reap. Let's discuss two possibilities why this might happen.

Poor or Incomplete Sowing

Sowing is a process that doesn't end with the actual sowing but requires follow-up. Those who sow must keep at it until the harvest, which generally takes awhile. Those who sow but fail to take care of the plantation may not have anything to reap. The Law of Sowing also states that not all the seeds we plant will bear fruit. And that's why we should use as many seeds as possible and tend our garden well.

Sowing poorly will have no result. Sowing on shallow ground and not watering your seeds are technical mistakes that can ruin all your crops. Success is a combination of factors—sowing is one of them, but it isn't everything.

Remember the Law of Wisdom: working is not enough. You need competence and intelligence to work well. The Law of Wisdom also teaches us that every sowing process involves some percentage of failure. It's our job to deal with the obstacles with persistence and resilience. Trying and failing are steps on the ladder to success. When we fail, we can learn from our mistakes and begin again in a more effective way.

Jesus warns us of this in his parable of the sower (see Matt. 13:1–9; Mark 4:1–9). A farmer went out to sow his seed. Some of the seeds were eaten by birds; some fell in shallow ground and were burned by the sun. Others were suffocated by thorns. But some fell in good soil, and they grew and bore much fruit.

Sowing requires proper techniques and good ground. Some loss or failure is inherent in the process. As time goes by, however, you will reap more due to your experience and personal and intellectual growth.

Overlapped Sowing

Why do some people sow seeds but don't reap crops? Sometimes there is nothing wrong with the sowing itself. Other factors may be involved. It is not a simple equation. Your reaping will be influenced not only by what you sow but by what others have sown before you or are currently sowing.

Our lives are affected not only by our sowing but also by the sowing of our families, our cities, our countries, and our planet. If you sow good seed but the city in which you live sows bad seed, it will be more difficult to reap good things and live well. A good example is a political election: you may choose a decent candidate, but if the majority chooses an inept one, you and everyone else will have to deal with his lack of leadership skills. The result each of us reaps is influenced by the environment we live in.

Someone who is very gifted can sow and fail to reap because of where he lives, while another less gifted but better located individual can have a promising harvest. Take the US Olympic team as an example. These athletes have more incentives and access to better conditions for practice, and that is often reflected in the medal count. Sometimes you have to deal with problems you did not create and reap something you did not plant. Hunger, violence, and disease are the results of what we as a society have been sowing for decades, centuries even. A person's good and bad actions will have repercussions on others, for we are all connected.

The prophet Jeremiah writes to the Jews, taken as slaves and sent to Babylon, these words from God: "Seek the peace and prosperity of the city to which I have carried you into exile. Pray to the LORD for it, because if it prospers, you too will prosper" (Jer. 29:7).

The Law of Sowing says that what happens today can be a result of seeds that have been sown throughout history. Complaining is pointless. This spiritual law is a matter of cause and effect and a reality that collectively affects us all.

What to Do Then?

> Turn from evil and do good; then you will dwell in the land forever. (Ps. 37:27)

Individually and as a society, we need to stop sowing bad things and start sowing good things and stand our ground until the evil that was sown in the past gives way to good. This is likely to take awhile.

We need to sow goodness—and we must do it well and consistently. We cannot just take out the weeds. We need to sow generously, not just sparingly: "Remember this: Whoever sows sparingly will also reap sparingly, and whoever sows generously will also reap generously" (2 Cor. 9:6). We need to properly care for our gardens and convince our neighbors to do the same for theirs. After all, bad seeds can blow in and take root. Actively care for your community, your country, and the planet because, like it or not, you are part of something larger than yourself, and you will be affected by other people's actions.

Sow what you want to reap in the future. Remember, those who sow corn will not harvest peas or rice or soybeans. The relation of cause and effect is undeniable.

Plant properly, and you will enjoy a good harvest. Though difficulties may arise, life will be better for you than for those who do nothing or sow bad seeds.

This book was written with the certainty that if you sow wisdom, work, values, relationships, and personal growth, you will reap better things for your life. People who sow will certainly reap more than those who dare not even dream or act.

We can and should sow with those around us. Teamwork increases the chances of success. If we do that and behave with discipline, intelligence, and integrity, we will be taking full advantage of the Law of Sowing. By sowing good seeds and tending to the soil, you will enjoy a plentiful harvest.

"Do not judge, and you will not be judged. Do not condemn, and you will not be condemned. Forgive, and you will be forgiven. Give, and it will be given to you. A good measure, pressed down, shaken together and running over, will be poured into your lap. For with the measure you use, it will be measured to you."

LUKE 6:37–38

PART 6

The Seven Cardinal Sins against Success

Now that you understand the twenty-five biblical laws of success, it will be helpful to deconstruct some myths and clear your mind of certain psychological barriers and traps that could prevent you from obtaining success.

When people improperly analyze the Bible or history and culture, it leads to misinterpretation and mistakes. And those mistakes can shackle people to a life of stagnation and failure. They can also shackle a country.

In Brazil there is some degree of repulsion against personal, professional, and financial advancement. It is almost the opposite of what is believed in the United States, where one of the major elements of its development was the mind-set that with hard work and the Lord's blessing, a better life is possible for anyone.

It's a simple matter: our home country of Brazil does not have a culture dedicated to work. People are almost angry with those who get ahead in life. They believe wealth to be a symptom of something wrong and that succeeding in life is a matter of luck, cheating, or marriage rather than education and hard work. Thus, their relationship with success and wealth becomes perverse, translating into disgust, guilt, and excess of ambition, instead of the ideal, which is searching for harmony and balance.

If you are a religious person, you need to be aware of some mistakes that may occur within churches, tending either to the "theology of prosperity" or to the "theology of poverty." The most common errors are:

- Thinking that God has to bestow blessings and wealth on those who go to church or make generous offerings;
- Thinking that it's wrong to want success or money; thinking that to want a better life and to prosper is a sin, is ugly, or is a sign of materialism;
- Considering wealth and money as somehow "dirty";
- Being unable to distinguish positive ambition (the desire to grow and improve one's life) from selfish ambition, which is criticized in the Bible;
- Waiting for God to provide without having to do anything in order to obtain success and prosperity.

If you hope to prosper, you have to watch out for misguided concepts, whether they are religious or not. In this final section, we will discuss the most common mistakes committed in the pursuit of success, which we have called "the seven cardinal sins against success" in a clear reference to the seven cardinal sins presented in the Bible.

Cardinal Sins	Cardinal Sins against Success
Gluttony	Haste
Avarice	Avarice
Lust	Not enjoying your work
Wrath	Anger against wealth
Jealousy	Jealousy or covetousness
Sloth	Sloth
Pride or vainglory	Pride

Since you have learned the twenty-five biblical laws of success and are eager to begin your journey to success, it is important to understand and unravel each of these sins in order to prevent them from slowing—or even stopping—your pursuit of success.

26

The Sin of Haste

Better a patient person than a warrior.

Proverbs 16:32

The first cardinal sin in the Bible is gluttony, which is the insatiable desire—over and beyond needs—for food, drink, or drugs. The biblical sin of gluttony can be seen in the professional world when people pursue success through the Sin of Haste. This sin is the haste to have success—and once success is achieved, the inability to be satisfied with enough.

In order to build a career or a business, haste and illusions are useless. Success takes time. It causes pain and it isn't easy. On the other hand, we can put your mind to rest regarding one thing: success is less harmful and less time-consuming than not being successful, quitting, or not having dreams or plans and sitting on the sidelines of life.

One of the wealthiest men on earth, Warren Buffett, once stated, "No matter how great the talent or efforts, some things just take time. You can't produce a baby in one month by getting nine women pregnant."[1] In other words, patience is an indispensable virtue for any professional or entrepreneur.

Keep in mind that it doesn't matter how long it takes, the sooner you start applying the twenty-five biblical laws of success, the sooner you will get there. It's a painful process but well worth it. Asking people for their opinions and honest appraisals, giving them the liberty to tell you the truth, and listening to your work being criticized take courage and willpower, and not everyone can handle it. But those who can will improve, because they get information about what and where to make changes. Seeking feedback and listening to criticism, and learning to distinguish between comments that are pertinent and those that can be ignored, are sometimes difficult, but they are the only way to improve.

To avoid the Sin of Haste, it is important to know that the best option won't be the easiest or quickest. When it comes to success, as the basketball phenomenon Michael Jordan would say, "There are no shortcuts,"[2] and those who show only partial effort face the risk of only partial results, or none whatsoever. It's like saying, "If you think education is expensive, wait till you see the price of ignorance." Haste is expensive. Wise people understand that the right direction is more important than speed.

The clearest manifestation of the haste for success arises when the subject is compensation. Many want to earn a high salary from day one and to be made CEO almost the day after being hired as an administrative assistant.

When looking for an internship or an entry-level job, it is a mistake to focus on the paycheck rather than on the opportunities for growth and learning. It's better to earn less (or nothing at all) in a place where you can learn a lot than to earn a lot in a place that teaches you nothing. The same applies to higher-level professionals.

Be in no hurry for a promotion or for the quick buck. The natural order of success is this: first you work hard, and then you become successful; first you find fulfillment, and then you worry about money; first you sow, and then you harvest. In our experience, those who want money first and rush to get rich quick don't get very far. On the other hand, those who focus on doing a good job, who are dream-driven, and who work hard to accomplish their goals will thrive.

One of the Bible's fundamental concepts is service, not wealth. Have you noticed that the world's most successful people are those who focus on their work, on their dreams, on their vocation, and on doing things that are useful? Throughout history great people, such as Henry Ford and Steve Jobs, have achieved success through revolutionary vision and hard work. Therefore, don't focus on money but on competence and dedication. Equip yourself with the qualities that breed success. Money will be a consequence.

Some say that money breeds money. We would say that money and work breed money. Saying that money will breed more money is a fallacy—this principle applies only if you handle money with knowledge and care. Money without wisdom breeds poverty, if all you do is spend it. Smart work that is fueled by competence, innovation, and dignity is the moneymaking machine. Competence is often more a matter of effort—accepting the challenge, studying, and developing skills—than it is a result of natural talent.

Money can also breed money when you carefully make legitimate investments and get a return on your investment. However, it is important to stress that one can become wealthy without a lot of capital, simply by hard work. The more competent and skilled you are, the greater the opportunities to earn more.

The important thing is not to be in a hurry to obtain success, whether professional or financial, without first creating a solid foundation of competence and hard work. The Bible tells us, "One eager to get rich will not go unpunished" (Prov. 28:20). A person who desires to get rich quick is committing the cardinal Sin of Haste against success and adopting a negative attitude; he or she is subject to its consequences. This is a matter of cause and effect.

Those in a hurry to achieve success and get wealth often end up closing bad deals. Haste shatters serenity, clouds reasoning, and causes people to make bad or ethically compromised decisions. In the professional world, those out for a quick buck usually end up in trouble. The Bible cautions us not to be in a hurry to get rich. This is valuable advice. If you want to make it in life—build a business, pass a test, become wealthy—accept that it takes time. In fact, in any important decision, from a real estate deal to choosing a spouse, haste is the enemy of wisdom and good choices.

If you are keen on becoming successful and making money, start getting ready right now. Act today. It will be easier to make more money in the future if you are working now and are a dedicated employee. Many people push success off to the future and never take this vital first step. They keep thinking, *When I switch jobs or when my work is appreciated, then I'll finally arrive on time; I'll do better.* If it's success you want, then you need to strive for excellence starting right now—even if you haven't yet reached the position you are aiming for, even if you haven't yet received the recognition you deserve or the salary of your dreams.

Personal progress through work is preceded by preparation, just like any construction job. Success requires planning, execution, and at all steps monitoring for occasional improvements and adjustments. Nobody makes it without having to sidestep obstacles that frequently appear when implementing a project. The more precious and the bolder the project, the more difficulties you will face, but the greater the prospect for results at the end of the day. And to make it to the finish line, you must be psychologically prepared to face tribulations along the way.

A very common mistake is to disregard the timeline. If you watch a shoe being polished, you may think that the shoe with the polish is uglier than the one without it. This is a case of optical illusion—shortsightedness as to what is and what could be. The shoe being polished will soon be shinier than the shoe that hasn't been polished.

Society associates success with money, titles, power, and fame. This is a misperception, as the Bible alerts: "A good name is more desirable than great riches" (Prov. 22:1). The real definition of *success* is having a good reputation, a good professional track record, and the results they produce for yourself, your family, and your place of work. Professional success arises when your employer begins to identify you as someone good to work with, with sound references; when your name is well referred to in the corporate world, among clients, and others. And this, dear reader, is worth more than what you can earn.

The more respected you are as a professional, the more clients and partners you will acquire, which will lead to more money. It's a simple rule that positive action leads to positive reaction. It's a virtuous cycle of constantly improving results. Promotions and money are a consequence.

Regarding the need for patience and gradual growth, it is worth reading what Jesus said about the growth of the kingdom of God, which is also applicable to professional life: "It is like a mustard seed, which is the smallest of all seeds on earth. Yet when planted, it grows and becomes the largest of all garden plants, with such big branches that the birds can perch in its shade" (Mark 4:31–32). Avoid the Sin of Haste by making your career the mustard seed that starts slowly and grows in a healthy and sustainable manner until it becomes a huge plant. Don't rush.

Antidotes to the Sin of Haste

- Cultivate patience.
- Transform what appear to be delays into opportunities to learn and gain experience.
- Remember that the right direction is more important than the speed.

Patience is bitter, but its fruit is sweet.
JEAN JACQUES ROUSSEAU

27

The Sin of Avarice

For the love of money is a root of all kinds of evil. Some
people, eager for money, have wandered from the faith
and pierced themselves with many griefs.

1 TIMOTHY 6:10

The biblical sin of avarice is an excessive attraction to money. But
when it comes to sins against success, the cardinal sin we want to
deal with is the perverse relationship with money: either we attribute too much value to it or we despise it, as we briefly discussed
in the opening of part 6. This is the Sin of Avarice.

Wealth is not synonymous with *happiness*, nor is *poverty* a syn-
onym of *unhappiness*. One thing that is worse than being poor is
being rich without being ready for it. Wealth can become a major
problem if it is not guided by principles or, for the lack of a better
word, maturity. Emotional stability is a must-have when dealing
with success and wealth, not to mention the ability to manage them.

It is often said that money can't buy happiness, and although that is true, you do not live off of happiness alone. You can't pay the utility bill with a bag of joy or deal with health-care expenses with just a smile. Money has its uses, and nothing beats it when it comes to paying for day-to-day expenses.

However, there are those who are convinced that money brings happiness, and they will do virtually anything to have lots of it, even if it involves corruption, fraud, and dishonesty. Those are the ones seduced by appearances. Wealth impresses people. It grants advantages, arranges marriages, mobilizes disciples, indicates solutions, and buys comfort. Nelson Rodrigues, a famous Brazilian novelist, quipped that "money buys everything, even true love."[1] That isn't true, but many people seem to believe so.

If money by itself were capable of ensuring everything that people need to feel happy and successful, we wouldn't see so many depressed or unfulfilled rich people. Money buys medication, but not health; it buys a house, but not a home. Even so, there are poor and middle-class people who believe they will be happy if they become wealthy.

We have to be careful not to attribute too much value to money nor too little. What does the Bible teach us about this? First, we shouldn't fall in love with money, and second, it shouldn't be a priority in our lives. We can have money, even lots of it, but we must handle it wisely. Money is a good slave but a bad master (Matt. 6:24–27; Luke 16:14).

Learn to have a healthy relationship with success and money, neither loving them nor disdaining them. Only then will they serve you well. As Socrates has said: "He who is not contented with what he has, would not be contented with what he would like to have."

Antidotes to the Sin of Avarice

- Develop a healthy relationship with money; don't be a miser or a spendthrift; avoid both greed and squander.
- Acquire principles and maturity to manage your wealth with balance.
- Don't consider money a priority in your life.
- Don't try to build a fortune at all costs, using dishonorable means.

Command those who are rich in this present world not to be arrogant nor to put their hope in wealth, which is so uncertain, but to put their hope in God, who richly provides us with everything for our enjoyment. Command them to do good, to be rich in good deeds, and to be generous and willing to share.

1 TIMOTHY 6:17–18

28

The Sin of Not Enjoying Your Work

Rejoice always.

1 THESSALONIANS 5:16

Lust is the passionate and selfish desire for all sensual and material pleasure. When it comes to professional success, the sin lies in precisely the opposite: not enjoying your work. The Sin of Not Enjoying Your Work is when you feel and seek pleasure only in leisure activities and are incapable of showing joy or passion for your work. As a result, your work is lacking in love, dedication, and care.

Don't make an effort to find pleasure; instead, learn to take pleasure from effort. Those who behave according to this principle get ahead in life. Those who take pleasure from working are more productive. However, many people don't enjoy working. Some work only out of obligation, while others are capable of discovering reasons for working. Of course we don't always do what we like, but we have to learn to like our job in order to do our work more effectively and more naturally.

Many people say that if they won the lottery the first thing they would do is quit their jobs. Little do they know that a few years after hitting the jackpot, most lottery winners are financially worse off than before. What's the use of winning a lot of money if we don't know how to manage it or invest it? As Solomon says, "Why should fools have money in hand to buy wisdom, when they are not able to understand it?" (Prov. 17:16).

There are studies pointing to lack of money management skills, or mismanagement, as the main cause of a poor financial record,[1] which is observable with lottery winners who spent the money recklessly and lost the prize in a short period of time. We might risk saying that if the world's entire wealth were divided equally among everyone, within a few years it would be back in the hands of those who are managing it well today. Why? Because they are people who know how to manage and create wealth, and they are repaid in kind. Those who don't know how to handle money wisely usually waste it in a jiffy. In that same vein, an American millionaire—who owned railroads, steel mills, and farms—is attributed as saying that he wouldn't mind losing everything he had if he could keep his health and his employees. According to him, he and his team would recover all he lost because it is people, not things, who create wealth and prosperity.

In spite of this there are people doing everything they can not to work, who never pick up a book or attend a lecture to learn something new. Personal advancement is achieved through studying (books, courses, lectures), apprenticeship (coexistence and observation), or one's own experience (hands-on, by trial and error). There is no other way.

The idea that work is punishment is inherent in our culture and may have arisen from an erroneous interpretation of the Bible—or at least the lack of the full meaning of Genesis 3:17–19. Here we read that Adam sinned and thereafter had to work and earn his bread by the sweat of his brow, which could lead to the conclusion that work was a punishment for his sin and therefore something bad. Many forget that before the fall Adam already had a job (Gen. 2:15).

In the New Testament work is praised by Jesus himself: "My Father is always at his work to this very day, and I too am working" (John 5:17). Jesus would never have referred to God as executing a punitive or cursed task. We trust in the wisdom of Psalm 128, which stresses that a blessed person lives by the work of his or her hands.

Live, then, by your own work. Try not to depend on others, whether it's the government, a former spouse, or a relative. If you aren't yet fond of working, learn to like it. Work is one of the most precious concepts in the Bible. It comes up again and again in this book, because God works through those working or willing to work. Seeking pleasure in work involves both being happy that we have a job and being happy while we are getting it done.

The Bible states, "The sun rises. . . . Then people go out to their work, to their labor until evening" (Ps. 104:22–23). These verses refer to people who start work early and work until late, and this comes across as something good. The following verse gives the impression that this is a kind of wealth: "How many are your works, Lord! In wisdom you made them all; the earth is full of your creatures" (Ps. 104:24). And it is indeed!

Seeing work as something good is one of the first steps toward enjoying it and benefiting from it. A good friend of ours, Ivo Ribeiro Restier, a successful businessman, owner of a school with thousands of students, says that he began his life as a waiter in a hotel in Rio de Janeiro. From that point on he considered each job a privilege and an opportunity in which he always tried to do his very best. With every new job, the same pleasure in accomplishing his tasks repeated itself. This is how one sows growth and success.

A happy person is good company. There is no boss, employee, or coworker who doesn't like a joyful person.

Antidotes to the Sin of Not Enjoying Your Work

- Think about your work's value in order to feel motivated. If you deal with clients, think about the good service you can deliver to them. If you are a blue-collar worker, imagine the customer's satisfaction with the product you've made.
- Every job comes with knowledge and benefits; sooner or later opportunities will emerge.
- The better you work, the bigger your chances of growth.

Your work is going to fill a large part of your life, and the only way to be truly satisfied is to do what you believe is great work. And the only way to do great work is to love what you do.

STEVE JOBS

29

The Sin of Anger
against Wealth

Abram had become very wealthy in livestock and in
silver and gold.

Genesis 13:2

There are those who believe it is wrong to get rich or improve in
life. They are even angry with those seeking prosperity. This attitude will ultimately reflect on their own success. If you think being
rich is bad, you will have problems dedicating yourself to getting
ahead in life. To make matters worse, when you commit the Sin
of Anger against Wealth, and you do achieve success, you will feel
guilty. It's very common for people to sabotage themselves while
seeking success and prosperity.

We've already said that our home country of Brazil is prejudiced
against wealth, to the point that external signs of wealth are seen
as indications of dishonesty and corruption instead of something

admirable, the fruit of labor and personal effort. Within the Brazilian collective subconscious, there is a series of wrong concepts that create resentment against the rich. When people finally achieve success, they quite often experience a guilt complex.

The rich are labeled as selfish and are seen as people who only achieved success by subterfuge, a marriage of convenience, or hitting the jackpot. There is even a widespread feeling that success, work, or wealth drives a wedge between the person and his or her family. Culturally there is a lot of resentment against those who make it in life. As Tom Jobim, a virtuoso Brazilian musician, would say, "In Brazil, success is a personal offense."[1]

These concepts are all dreadfully wrong! Of course there are dishonest and selfish rich people, but wealth is not the reason. Dysfunctional families exist everywhere, and fraud is everywhere too. Have you never heard of someone with a fake ID? It's interesting to observe how many people think that when a rich person is dishonest he's a thief and when a poor person is dishonest he's a poor little thing, a victim, a person in need.

This prejudice is explained by the Sin of Anger against Wealth— people allege that excessive resources make rich people behave unethically. Ethical dilemmas are not the prerogative of those who have fortunes, though economic power often means that many wealthy people escape the clutches of the law, contributing to the stereotype. For there to be progress, society must treat crimes as crimes, regardless of their perpetrators, leaving no room for corruption and impunity. There has been a movement in Brazil requesting transparency and efficiency from our institutions. This reveals change is on its way; the population is gradually becoming intolerant to scams and corruption.

The question here is: Do you harbor any of these prejudices or mental barriers against wealth? If so, you need to get rid of them. The prejudice against wealth is one of the sins that one may commit while trying to succeed.

There are good, generous rich people who achieved success thanks to their competence and dedication and who use their wealth with dignity, honesty, and for the good of their families and others. Acquiring these mental models of achievement and finding admirable paradigms is part of the process of motivation and guidance for success.

What Are the Origins of This Prejudice against Wealth?

> Command those who are rich in this present world not to be arrogant nor to put their hope in wealth, which is so uncertain, but to put their hope in God, who richly provides us with everything for our enjoyment. (1 Tim. 6:17)

For a long time the order of the day was, "To be poor is beautiful, wealth is shameful, and work is punishment." In addition to the historical and cultural reasons already mentioned there is another supposedly religious origin that arises from a misinterpretation of biblical teaching. In Matthew 19:24 Jesus says, "It is easier for a camel to go through the eye of a needle than for someone who is rich to enter the kingdom of God." This is why many people conclude that being rich is dangerous or undesirable. But a couple of verses later, Jesus goes on to say, "With man this is impossible, but with God all things are possible" (v. 26). This means that a rich man can indeed enter the kingdom of heaven. In this part of the Bible Jesus is drawing attention to a fundamental aspect that the rich have to overcome.

Mark 10:17–22 is another passage from the Bible that is usually misunderstood as it relates to the concept of wealth. A rich young man asks Jesus what he should do in order to inherit eternal life. Jesus tells the young man that he should sell all his belongings and give to the poor. The issue in this passage is not money itself but rather the greedy attitude the young man has toward his possessions. Jesus notices this attitude and gives him an opportunity to repent of it. He has the choice of following the advice or not.

If prospering from work was evil, there would have been no recommendation to enjoy your work, as we see in Ecclesiastes 5:18, "This is what I have observed to be good: that it is appropriate for a person to eat, to drink and to find satisfaction in their toilsome labor under the sun during the few days of life God has given them—for this is their lot."

By the way, the Bible has several pieces of advice for the rich. None of these recommends that people forgo their wealth but rather that they manage their money correctly and in a generous manner, that they be honest and humble, and that they not place their trust in the uncertainties of wealth (1 Tim. 6:17–19; Eph. 6:9; Mark 10:17–22).

Those who despise success and blame the rich for all of society's woes are also committing the Sin of Anger against Wealth. The elite may be guilty of many things but are not solely responsible. And let's not confuse the privileged elite with anyone who makes money or improves his or her lot in life.

As a matter of fact, one of the best ways to change society is precisely by creating opportunities for education, work, entrepreneurship, and social advancement. Wealth is not to blame for poverty; instead, social inequality born of historical and current issues is to blame. The huge void between the social classes we see in our home country of Brazil took years to come about. This scenario, it should be noted, is also the result of a series of public and private measures that violate the principles of the Bible. To say that Brazil is a Christian nation is only partly accurate, since the majority of government, private companies, and individuals do not abide by the guidelines in the Bible or those given by Jesus.

Nothing explains or justifies the jealousy or persecution of the wealthy. Actually, this is the first step to remaining in poverty. After all, someone who feels jealousy, resentment, or hatred toward someone who is successful is not on the path to success. These are not constructive feelings.

If you want to get ahead in life, start to admire and bless those who are successful in life, who work hard, and who study and work in an honest manner. If you are a Christian and fail to do this, your anger against wealth will not only affect your success on the secular level but will also contradict the religious principles of loving your neighbor and not coveting or grumbling.

Another aspect of failing to admire success is the addiction to poverty. There are those who believe it is commendable and good to be poor. Because they are angry with the rich or with how some have achieved their wealth, some people come to like being poor.

Being poor is neither a shame nor a problem. There are poor people who have more dignity and who are happier than many millionaires. The problem is that some now encourage and admire poverty as if it were a virtue, attributing to poverty a moral or philosophical aspect that it does not have.

There are social and intellectual environments that appear to put the culture of poverty on a pedestal. This happens in some churches, for example. If poverty is found to be a virtue, it will be admired and the status preserved. It's one thing to respect a poor person; it's another thing to think you have to remain in poverty.

Some intellectuals claim that people who are poor enjoy greater purity, innocence, candor, or goodness. That's not the case: good and evil can be found across all social, educational, and economic levels. In the religious arena, we have noticed that humility, a virtue, is often confused with poverty.

Mahatma Gandhi, in his autobiography, talks about a wealthy friend named Raychandbhai:

> Raychandbhai's commercial transactions covered hundreds of thousands. He was a connoisseur of pearls and diamonds. No knotty business problem was too difficult for him. But all these things were not the centre round which his life revolved. That centre was the passion to see God face to face. Amongst the things on his business table there were invariably to be found some religious book and his diary. The moment he finished his business he opened the religious book or the diary. Much of his published writings is a reproduction from this diary. The man who, immediately on finishing his talk about weighty business transaction[s], began to write about the hidden things of the spirit could evidently not be a businessman at all, but a real seeker after Truth.[2]

This passage shows that one can be both rich and successful, noble and spiritual, at the same time.

Antidotes to the Sin of Anger against Wealth

- Choose as your role models wealthy and successful people who deserve your admiration because they are honest, generous, and hard workers.

- Don't be ashamed of wishing for a better life.
- Set yourself free from believing it is more honorable to be poor than rich.
- Think of all the good things you can give to your loved ones and others if you prosper.

If you are ashamed of your goal you will never achieve it.
ROBERTO SHINYASHIKI

30

The Sin of Jealousy or Covetousness

The stingy are eager to get rich and are unaware that poverty awaits them.

PROVERBS 28:22

Covetousness is to desire what others have, and it is condemned in the Ten Commandments (Exod. 20:17). Jealousy is even worse, because what other people have bothers us. Deep down, in both cases, the person becomes attached to what is not theirs, either because they want it for themselves (greed/covetousness) or because they don't want the other person to have it (jealousy). These are both extremely negative and harmful sentiments. To avoid these feelings the best antidote is detachment.

One of the greatest barriers to success is to be jealous of others instead of working toward your own dreams. When the Bible says that jealous people will become poor, it is not because God will punish them, but simply because they will experience the effects of wasting their energy on that which results in nothing.

When William wrote his first book, *Como Passar em Provas e Concursos* (*How to Pass Tests and Public Examinations*), in 1998, he wrote that jealousy can be a large stone in the shoe of someone wanting to pass a test. He recommended that students avoid the urge to complain, to present themselves as victims, or to look for someone or something to blame.

Years later, when reading the book *Secrets of the Millionaire Mind* by T. Harv Eker, one particular part caught his attention, an excerpt that says jealousy gets in the way of those who want to be a millionaire. The book corrects many misconceptions about wealth.[1] Why does it mention jealousy? Because jealous people focus their attention on the wrong things. They waste their energy on what is not essential. Adolfo Martins, a Brazilian journalist and media tycoon, frequently says that he became successful because he focused on positive and productive actions and emotions.[2]

Jealousy leads people to waste money and exploit the belongings of others, instead of looking after their own. The biblical command against covetousness is so that people will mind their own business, which is more productive than complaining about what they do not have.

There is a parable in the Gospel of Matthew that tells the story of a generous owner who paid good salaries even to those who worked only a few hours. Those who worked all day complained, despite having received the agreed-upon payment. The issue here is the uncomfortable realization that those who work less earn the same. Notice what the owner says at the end: "Don't I have the right to do what I want with my own money? Or are you envious because I am generous?" (Matt. 20:15).

Jealousy of someone else and what they have is the same mistake those workers made—namely, caring about the good things others have received. Instead, focus on what you have and be thankful. Tend to your own life, and do not be envious of others.

This also applies to what your coworkers earn. That is not your concern. Yours is to improve professionally, so that you can experience the positive results of your efforts.

Antidotes to the Sin of Jealousy or Covetousness

- Focus your energy on your work and on your own positive ambitions.
- Strive for what you desire; don't resent the effort you will have to put in and the things others possess.
- Sincerely enjoy when someone improves his or her lot in life, and take it as an encouragement.

A lot of people get so hung up on what they can't have that they don't think for a second about whether they really want it.

LIONEL SHRIVER

31

The Sin of Sloth

Laziness brings on deep sleep, and the shiftless go
hungry.

PROVERBS 19:15

People who commit the Sin of Sloth hope to earn their living the
same way the Jews gained food in the desert when God sent down
bread and quail for them to eat (Exod. 16). They expect God to
make job offers and money fall from the sky and to provide for
their living, so they don't have to step outside their comfort zone.
In other words, these are the ones who hope for a paycheck at the
end of each month without having to work for it. To these people,
the ideal position would be a four-hour-a-week job. They would
like to become the CEO of a great company, but would delegate
the hard work needed to the team.

Unfortunately, there is no easy way to earn money these days.
Neither is it possible to thrive without working hard and putting

in some effort. As the Bible says, "Those who work their land will have abundant food, but those who chase fantasies have no sense" (Prov. 12:11).

Lazy people don't stand a chance in the marketplace. As soon as their true nature is uncovered and a suitable replacement is found, they will be replaced. Solomon, known for his wisdom, talks against the Sin of Sloth in the book of Proverbs:

> Go to the ant, you sluggard;
>> consider its ways and be wise!
> It has no commander,
>> no overseer or ruler,
> yet it stores its provisions in summer
>> and gathers its food at harvest.
>
> How long will you lie there, you sluggard?
>> When will you get up from your sleep?
> A little sleep, a little slumber,
>> a little folding of the hands to rest—
> and poverty will come on you like a thief
>> and scarcity like an armed man. (6:6–11)

The picture Solomon paints about sloth isn't flattering. A person who seeks excuses to abstain from work isn't wise. On the contrary, he will become a hassle and a source of frustration for those who depend on him. A slothful person is proud and arrogant: "A sluggard is wiser in his own eyes than seven people who answer discreetly" (Prov. 26:16). He dreams of winning the lottery, having a million-dollar idea, or being recruited by a headhunter, but despite his lofty wishes he is an underachiever. The ending to his story is not surprising:

> I went past the field of a sluggard,
>> past the vineyard of someone who has no sense;
> thorns had come up everywhere,
>> the ground was covered with weeds,
>> and the stone wall was in ruins.
> I applied my heart to what I observed
>> and learned a lesson from what I saw:
> A little sleep, a little slumber,
>> a little folding of the hands to rest—
> and poverty will come on you like a thief
>> and scarcity like an armed man. (Prov. 24:30–34)

There are people who believe in achieving a bright future without any effort; others dream about the future in order to escape their day-to-day responsibilities. In order to become reality, dreams must come with plans and effort or they will be only illusions.

To turn dreams into reality, we cannot be slothful. We must plan, organize, and plow the land. In their fantasies, dreamers imagine miraculous solutions for their problems, but these solutions will likely require some luck and the help of others. Dreamers often leave unfinished projects along the way, because they are not doers. When the execution part begins—the hands-on hard work—the dreamer moves on to a larger, more spectacular fantasy!

Here are a few questions to ask yourself, then: Have you been working the land? If you are in college, are you studying? Are you committed to your studies? Are you committed to improving your performance reviews at work? As a businessman, are you constantly recycling your knowledge, searching for new and better ways to conduct your business? As the Bible says, have you been giving "careful attention to your herds" (Prov. 27:23)? Have you given any thought to your business plan? Are you aware of your strengths and weaknesses? Do you know how to manage them in order to succeed?

In one of Joyce Meyer's messages, she points out the importance of working and sowing:

> The problem is, some people want to win but don't want to go through the struggle; they want to be prosperous but do not want to sow; they want to improve their financial life, but they are not willing to do what is needed, such as help others.
>
> Sometimes you have to take a step back to gain momentum to move forward.... We can't have it both ways. This is the truth. There will be things in life that you don't care for or you don't want to do but have to, and believe it or not, this is healthy. Because if we had everything our way, if we did only what we want, if there was no opposition, if everything was a given, and there was nothing else to conquer, you know what we would be? We would be a bunch of spoiled children. Sometimes you need to feel uncomfortable in order to change places.[1]

Are you dreaming or stagnating? One of the worst varieties of sloth is when people don't realize they are standing still. People can lose themselves in dreams and elaborate expectations and not set anything in motion. Roberto Shinyashiki indicates, "It is not important where you come from nor how you are right now. What is life-determining is your ability to make your dreams come true."[2] Those who have many dreams and fantastic ideas may end up less successful and fulfilled than those who are less creative but more hands-on.

The Bible is wary of those who seek fantasies instead of working the land. Dreams without commitment are fantasies. What separates the dreaming fool from the successful dreamer is that the latter is also a doer while the former merely fantasizes. The fool lacks discipline and action to bring his dreams to life. A dream should prompt movement, not stagnation.

Antidotes to the Sin of Sloth

- Start to discipline yourself. Build a schedule to determine actions and deadlines and stick to it.
- Think of the fruits you will reap when you overcome sloth and start working toward your dreams.
- Don't wait for opportunities to fall into your lap or wonder what life would be like if you won the lottery or had that million-dollar idea.
- Get to work.

> *Sloth is the failure to do what needs to be done when it needs to be done.*
> JOHN ORTBERG

32

The Sin of Pride

Before a downfall the heart is haughty, but humility comes before honor.

PROVERBS 18:12

The Sin of Pride manifests itself when a person thinks he or she is better than others, failing to respect his or her neighbors and walking all over people. Unfortunately, vanity and arrogance are quite common; there is even a popular expression about success going to your head. It's worse when those who have only just begun to climb the ladder of life show an utter lack of humility.

There are various symptoms of this issue, including judging yourself better than others, disdaining those around you, and spending too much money. One clear sign of pride and vanity is flaunting (or faking) a social status by spending more than you earn on shallow possessions, luxurious and expensive trifles, and symbols of power. Even when you have the money, flaunting it is not right.

The Bible says that pride precedes a fall (Prov. 16:18) and that every mountain will be made low (Isa. 40:4). Be humble, so that hard-won success doesn't turn against you, adversely affecting your current and future growth. Besides attracting everyone's admiration and kindness, humility is a requirement for continued growth.

There is a Chinese proverb that says, "When the game ends, the king and the pawn go back into the same box." Humility never hurt anyone and is important in professional life. Learn to be humble, not in an exaggerated or fake manner but from the heart, for you know that humility is one of the best defenses against jealousy and errors of judgment.

In his book *The Servant,* James Hunter develops the concept of servant leadership based on the wisdom of Jesus, as seen in this passage:

> Jesus called them together and said, "You know that the rulers of the Gentiles lord it over them, and their high officials exercise authority over them. Not so with you. Instead, whoever wants to become great among you must be your servant." (Matt. 20:25–26)

Inspired by the Bible's wisdom, Hunter claims that respect, responsibility, and caring for people are underlying virtues of a good leader. And in order to become a good leader it is necessary to be willing to serve, which is incompatible with someone who is arrogant and believes that he or she is solely responsible for a business's success.[1]

You might question, "But how can someone who serves get ahead in life?" In fact, servants are the most desirable assets in the job market. If you do not serve a purpose, you will have a hard time building a successful career or business.

Life is ephemeral, fragile, and surprising. Chance and change are part of the game: sometimes we are leaders; other times we are followers. Therefore, a dose of humility and flexibility is a welcome asset. An arrogant and pretentious person stands a lesser chance of predicting or adapting to the surprises that life and the market puts in his or her way.

Humility is insurance against many personal errors. Whether by analyzing history or out of reason or faith, being humble is a necessary asset to reaching and staying at the top.

Antidotes to the Sin of Pride

- Be humble; you will have much more to gain if you are not arrogant.
- Respect and value people who work for you and with you.
- Remember: pride precedes a fall.
- Never forget: you may be on top today, but tomorrow you may fall.
- You must be willing to serve in order to become a leader.

Success often leads to arrogance, and arrogance to failure.
AL REIS AND JACK TROUT

Conclusion

Beyond Secular Success—This Madness Called Jesus

We are in daily contact with all kinds of people—successful and not quite so successful entrepreneurs, doctors, lawyers, freelancers, bricklayers, beauticians, janitors, housekeepers—and in all levels we find good and bad people. We believe it is always good to share our experiences and encourage people to discover the power of the twenty-five biblical laws of success. But we cannot end this book without saying that the Bible goes far beyond professional and financial success. Jesus himself was born in a stable and "had no place to lay his head" (Matt. 8:20; Luke 9:58).

The highest form of success is to comprehend the revolutionary paradigm that Jesus brought to us when he spoke about his kingdom, which is very different from the kingdoms on earth. Jesus's ideas were considered madness by many. They were inconvenient because he talked about love and relationships in a way that also favored the poor and the meek. That is a concept that most people are not prepared to understand. God loves all people, even the weak.

Jesus will always be a mystery for those who seek redemption by their own merit, wealth, or wisdom. For those who want to go it alone, who think they can make it on their own, and who believe they are fine without him, Jesus's ideas are uncomfortable. Jesus came for everyone, including the crazy, the misfits, and the unfit. Those who believe they are sane won't want Jesus.

We appreciate Jesus because he represents an alternative to what is offered by society and the market. He can take care of all of us, and not only the winners and the powerful. He is not here to save only the intelligent and the talented, those of noble birth, or self-made people. Jesus blesses equally the illiterate and the PhD, the poor person and the millionaire. You don't have to be as rich as Bill Gates nor as smart as Albert Einstein nor a prophet. You don't need to fit into society's standards in order to follow Jesus.

Jesus loves saints and sinners. He accepts drunks, fools, and the unemployed, as well as the rich and brilliant. He doesn't discriminate. We admire and respect the elite, the rich, the wise, the PhDs of the world, but we are devoted to a God who also helps the poor, the weak, and the unfortunate—those who did not attain success as defined by society.

The Bible says, "God chose the foolish things of the world to shame the wise; God chose the weak things of the world to shame the strong. God chose the lowly things of this world and the despised things—and the things that are not—to nullify the things that are" (1 Cor. 1:27–28). You may be intelligent, successful, or powerful. You may have properties, titles, and positions. But you should not believe you have an advantage over others or a spiritual privilege because of secular success. This alone is not enough to guarantee a connection with God. Neither will it make God love you more. The salvation offered through Jesus by faith in him is free. That makes us all equal before God.

Therefore Jesus is madness, a scandal, because he is calm and humble. He gives everyone simple and direct access to God. He breaks the paradigms of the secular world.

We hope that if you are capable of growing a fortune by your own merits, if you are smart and wise, that it doesn't build a wall between you and Jesus. Secular success can endure eighty to one hundred years at most. But the salvation that Jesus provides is forever. You don't have to be "the best" to be loved and saved by Jesus, to have Jesus by your side along the way, in this world and the next.

That's why we are devoted to Jesus and why we choose to serve him. We may not be the best servants—we wouldn't even call ourselves good servants—but we are sure, as Martin Luther King Jr. would say, we have come a long, long way. We admit, though, that we still have a long way to go in our relationships with Jesus, with others, and with ourselves.[1]

We hope the knowledge we have shared in this book—the laws, concepts, and principles—are of good use in your life. Let this book be the instrument you use to achieve or to increase your success. We would like to close, however, by saying that whatever your level of success, there is a loving God cheering for you and with big plans for your life.

> *What oxygen is to the lungs, hope is to our survival*
> *in this world. And the Bible is filled with hope.*
> Billy Graham

Notes

Introduction

1. Roberto Shinyashiki, *O Sucesso é ser Feliz* [Success is living happily] (São Paulo: Editora Gente, 2012).

Chapter 1 The Law of Opportunity

1. Napoleon Hill, *Think and Grow Rich* (1937; repr., Hollywood, FL: Simon & Brown, 2010), 82.

Chapter 4 The Law of Focus

1. Harvard Health, "Positive Thinking Seems to Help the Heart," *Chicago Tribune*, January 25, 2012, http://articles.chicagotribune.com/2012-01-25/health/sc-health -0125-heart-study-20120125_1_heart-disease-positive-emotions-emotional-health, accessed February 24, 2016.

Chapter 5 The Law of Planning

1. John C. Maxwell, *The 15 Invaluable Laws of Growth* (New York: Center Street, 2012); George Armitage Miller, Eugene Galanter, and Kal H. Pribram, *Plans and the Structure of Behavior* (New York: Adam Bannister Cox Pubs, 1996); Jamie Novak, *1000 Best Quick and Easy Organizing Secrets* (Naperville, IL: Sourcebooks, 2006); David Allen, *Getting Things Done: The Art of Stress-Free Productivity* (New York: Penguin, 2002).

2. *American Heritage Dictionary of the English Language*, 5th ed. (New York: Houghton Mifflin Harcourt, 2011), s.v., "prudence," http://www.thefreedictionary.com/prudence.

3. William Shakespeare, *Henry V*, act 3, scene 7, page 6.

4. Marc Macini, *Time Management* (New York: McGraw-Hill, 2003); Marc Macini, *Time Management: 24 Techniques to Make Each Minute Count at Work* (New York: McGraw-Hill,

2007); Alec Mackenzie and Pat Nickerson, *The Time Trap: The Classic Book on Time Management* (Saranac Lake, NY: AMACOM, 1997); B. Eugene Griessman, *Time Tactics of Very Successful People* (New York: McGraw-Hill, 2007).

Chapter 6 The Law of Work

1. M. J. Ryan, *Trusting Yourself: Growing Your Self-Awareness, Self-Confidence, and Self-Reliance* (New York: Harmony Books, 2004); Dr. Joseph Murphy, *Believe in Yourself* (Chicago: Snowball Publishing, 2012).

2. Hill, *Think and Grow Rich*.

3. Jorge Videira, *Do Monturo Deus Ergue um Vencedor* [From a dunghill God raises a winner] (Rio de Janeiro: Editora Betel, 2013).

4. *Elite Squad*, directed by José Padilha (New York: IFC Films, 2007). Movie based on the novel *A Elite da Tropa* [The elite of the troop] by Rodrigo Pimentel (Rio de Janeiro: Objetiva, 2006).

5. One of the ten Corporation Rules for the Batalhão de Operações Especiais (BOPE) of Rio de Janeiro, the Special Operations Unit which inspired the movie *Elite Squad*.

Chapter 7 The Law of Courage

1. Niccolò Machiavelli, *The Prince* (London: Grant Richards, 1903), 69–70.

2. Al Ries and Jack Trout, *The 22 Immutable Laws of Marketing* (New York: Harper-Collins, 1993), 2.

3. William Douglas, *Como Passar em Provas e Concursos* [How to pass tests and public examinations], 29th ed. (Niterói: Impetus, 2014). *Como Passar em Provas e Concursos* created a new subject matter currently on the syllabi of a number of prep courses in Brazil, with several teachers and subsidiary books dedicated to it.

4. Ralph Waldo Emerson, *The Early Lectures of Ralph Waldo Emerson*, vol. 2 (Cambridge, MA: Harvard University Press, 1964), 243.

5. Nick Vujicic, *Life Without Limits* (Colorado Springs: Waterbrook, 2012), 202.

Chapter 8 The Law of Resilience

1. Paul Stoltz, *Adversity Quotient: Turning Obstacles into Opportunities* (New York: John Wiley & Sons, 1997).

2. Claus Moller, *O Lado Humano da Qualidade* [The human side of quality] (São Paulo: Thompson Pioneira, 1999), 136.

3. William E. Deming, *The Plan, Do, Study, Act Cycle*, The W. Edwards Deming Institute, https://www.deming.org/theman/theories/pdsacycle, accessed February 24, 2016.

4. Robert Dilts, *Neuro-Linguistic Programming, Volume 1: The Study of the Structure of Subject Experience* (Capitola, CA: Meta Publications, 1980).

Chapter 9 The Law of Joy

1. Elena Alves Silva, "Passado e Presente na história das Mulheres" [Past and present of women's history], Universidade Metodista de São Paulo, http://portal.metodista.br/pastoral/reflexoes-da-pastoral/passado-e-presente-na-historia-das-mulheres.

Chapter 10 The Law of Recharging

1. Domenico De Masi, *L'Ozio Creativo: Conversazione con Maria Serena Palieri* [Creative idleness: Conversation with Maria Serena Palieri] (Rome: Ediesse, 1995).
2. "Dormir para Aprender" [Sleep to learn], *Veja magazine*, edition 2.035, November 21, 2007, https://acervo.veja.abril.com.br/index.html#/edition/2035?page=1&search ing=true&section=1&word=2035.

Chapter 11 The Law of Self-Hiring

1. Thomas C. Corley, *Rich Habits: The Daily Success Habits of Wealthy Individuals* (Minneapolis: Hillcrest Media Group, 2010).

Chapter 12 The Law of Honesty

1. Jacquelyn Smith, *This CEO Learned Her Hiring Strategy from Warren Buffett*, *Business Insider*, October 2, 2014, http://www.businessinsider.com/warren-buffett-hiring -strategy-2014-10.
2. Robert Half Management Resources, "Honesty Still the Best Policy: CFO Survey Finds Integrity Most Desired Leadership Quality," September 22, 2016, http://rh-us .mediaroom.com/2016-09-22-What-Is-The-Most-Important-Leadership-Attribute."
3. *Corruption Perceptions Index 2011*, Transparency International, http://www.trans parency.org/cpi2011/results.

Chapter 13 The Law of Names

1. Eduardo Couture, *Decalogue of the Attorney*, quoted in "The Attorney Ten Commandments and Ethical Standards," Iustitia.es, http://iustitia.es/confianza/?lang=en.
2. This quote is widely attributed to Abraham Lincoln, but some suggest it was originally said by Jacques Abbadie or Denis Diderot. See discussion and citations regarding the origin of this statement in Quote Investigator, December 11, 2013, http://quoteinvestigator .com/2013/12/11/cannot-fool/#more-7793.
3. Adilson Romualdo Neves, *Qualidade no Atendimento* [Quality service] (Rio de Janeiro: Qualitymark, 2006).
4. Adilson Romualdo Neves, "Branding como Ferramenta Gerencial da Marca nas Igrejas" [Branding as a management tool for churches], Instituto Jetro, March 20, 2010, http://www.institutojetro.com/Artigos/comunicacao-e-marketing/branding-como-fer ramenta-gerencial-da-marca-nas-igrejas.html.
5. Jane Pavitt, *Brand.New* (London: Princeton University Press, 2003), 224.
6. Jeffrey H. Dyer, *Collaborative Advantage: Winning Through Extended Enterprise Supplier Networks* (Oxford: Oxford University Press, 2000).
7. Tony Simons, "The High Cost of Lost Trust," *Harvard Business Review*, September 2000, https://hbr.org/2002/09/the-high-cost-of-lost-trust.

Chapter 14 The Law of the Company You Keep

1. Kathleen Elkins, "15 Quotes from Warren Buffett That Take You Inside the Mind of a Legendary Investor," *Business Insider*, October 10, 2015, http://www.businessinsider .com/warren-buffetts-greatest-quotes-2015-10.

Chapter 15 The Law of Self-Control

1. Napoleon Hill, "Lesson Four," in *The Law of Success in Sixteen Lessons* (Meriden, CT: Ralston University Press, 1928), 12.

2. Martin H. Manser, comp., *The Westminster Collection of Christian Quotations* (London: Westminster John Knox, 2001), 232.

Chapter 16 The Law of Love

1. Dr. Martin Luther King Jr., "A Christmas Sermon on Peace," delivered at Ebenezer Baptist Church, Atlanta, Georgia, on Christmas Eve 1967, http://www.thekingcenter.org/archive/document/christmas-sermon#.

2. Hill, "Lesson Sixteen," *Law of Success in Sixteen Lessons,* 35.

3. William Shakespeare, *Richard the Third,* act 5, scene 4, 7–10.

Chapter 17 The Law of Agreement

1. Baltasar Gracián, *The Art of Worldly Wisdom* (New York: Macmillan, 1904), 179.

2. Eduardo Almeida, "Panel: School and People Management: What Is the Ideal Way of Obtaining a Successful School?," *19º Educar–Congresso Internacional de Educação* [19th Educar International Congress of Education], São Paulo, 2012.

3. Catho, *Pesquisa dos Profissionais Brasileiros* [Brazilian professionals' research], 2013, http://img.catho.com.br/site/landing/pesquisa-executivos/2013/images/pdf/CATHO_Apres_2013.pdf.

Chapter 18 The Law of Usefulness

1. Laffer Curve, The Laffer Center, http://www.laffercenter.com/the-laffer-center-2/the-laffer-curve/.

2. Hill, "Lesson One," *Law of Success in Sixteen Lessons,* 18.

Chapter 19 The Law of Advice

1. Antônio Houaiss, *Dicionário da Língua Portuguesa* [Dictionary of Portuguese language] (São Paulo: Editora Objetiva, 2009), s.v. "feedback," eletronic edition.

2. Raul Candeloro, *Feedback,* Catho, http://www.catho.com.br/cursos/feedback.

3. Ibid.

4. Ebenézer Bittencourt, *Qual é o Tamanho dos Seus Sonhos?* [How great are your dreams?], 4th ed. (Santa Bárbara d'Oeste, São Paulo: Noutética Publicações Ltda., 2009), 48–49.

5. Ken Blanchard, *Princípios da Liderança* [Principles of leadership] (São Paulo: Garimpo Editorial, 2010), 13.

Chapter 20 The Law of Leadership

1. Carlos Wizard Martins, *Desperte o Milionário que Há em Você* [Awake the millionaire within you] (São Paulo: Editora Gente, 2012).

2. Ibid.

3. Sun Tzu, *The Art of War* (Argentina: Ediciones Lea S.A., 2015).

4. Antoine de Saint Exupéry, *O Pequeno Príncipe* [*The Little Prince*], 48th ed. (Rio de Janeiro: Agir, 2009), 38.

5. J. Oswald Sanders, *Spiritual Leader: Principles of Excellence for Every Believer* (Chicago: Moody, 2007), 13.

Chapter 22 The Law of Generosity

1. Carnegie Corporation of New York, "Andrew Carnegie's Story," https://www.car negie.org/interactives/foundersstory/#!/.

2. For more information and facts about the Giving Pledge, see http://givingpledge.org.

3. Helio Gurovitz and Nelson Blecher, "O Estigma do Lucro" [The profit stigma], *Exame Magazine*, March 23, 2005, http://exame.abril.com.br/revista-exame/edicoes/839 /noticias/o-estigma-do-lucro-m0040657.

4. Natura Brasil, Investor Relations, "The Company," http://natu.infoinvest.com.br /static/enu/a-empresa.asp?idioma=enu.

Chapter 23 The Law of Contentment

1. Max Gehringer, *Clássicos do Mundo Corporativo* [Corporate world classics] (São Paulo: Editora Globo, 2008), 97–98.

2. Ibid.

3. Shawn Achor, *The Happiness Advantage: The Seven Principles of Positive Psychology That Fuel Success and Performance at Work* (New York: Crown Business, 2010).

4. Laurence J. Peter, *A Competência ao Alcance de Todos: As Receitas de Peter (Como ser Criativo, Confidante e Competente)* [The Peter prescription: How to be creative, confident and competent], 4th ed. (Rio de Janeiro: José Olympio, 1994), 23, 24, 127.

Chapter 24 The Law of Employability

1. "3 Things Buffett Looks for in People," WarrenBuffett.com, February 3, 2014, http:// www.warrenbuffett.com/3-things-buffett-looks-for-in-people/.

Chapter 25 The Law of Sowing

1. Madeleine L'Engle, *A Wind in the Door* (New York: Square Fish, 2007), 134.

Chapter 26 The Sin of Haste

1. "The 16 Best Things Warren Buffett Has Ever Said," *Huffington Post*, August 30, 2013, http://www.huffingtonpost.com/2013/08/30/warren-buffett-quotes_n_3842509.html.

2. Michael Jordan, *Driven from Within* (New York: Atria Books, 2005), 1.

Chapter 27 The Sin of Avarice

1. Nelson Rodrigues, *A Flor da Obsessão* [The obsession flower] (São Paulo: Companhia das Letras, 1997), 53.

Chapter 28 The Sin of Not Enjoying Your Work

1. T. Harv Eker, *Secrets of the Millionaire Mind* (New York: HarperCollins, 2007); Thomas J. Stanley and William D. Danko, *The Millionaire Next Door* (Atlanta: Longstreet Press, 1997).

Chapter 29 The Sin of Anger against Wealth

1. Tom Jobim, in answer to the critics. See Stella Caymmi, *Dorival Caymmi: o Mar e o Tempo* [Dorival Caymmi: The sea and the time] (São Paulo: Editora 34, 2001), 185.

2. Mahatma Gandhi, *An Autobiography, or The Story of My Experiments with Truth* (Ahmedabad: Navajivan Publishing House, 1927), 1045.

Chapter 30 The Sin of Jealousy or Covetousness

1. Eker, *Secrets of the Millionaire Mind,* 86–94.

2. Adolfo Martins, *Discurso Proferido ao Receber o Título de Doutor* Honoris Causa *Outorgado pela Universidade Castelo Branco* [Acceptance speech from receiving the title of Doctor *Honoris Causa* from Castelo Branco University] (Rio de Janeiro: Editora do Educador, 2003).

Chapter 31 The Sin of Sloth

1. Joyce Meyer, *Homem Espiritual e o Discernimento* [Spiritual man and the knowledge] (Belo Horizonte: Alianca Dist., 2007), DVD.

2. Roberto Shinyashiki, *O Sucesso é ser Feliz* [Success is living happily] (São Paulo: Editora Gente, 1997), 132.

Chapter 32 The Sin of Pride

1. James C. Hunter, *The Servant* (Rocklin, CA: Prima, 1988), ix–xxxxii.

Conclusion

1. Martin Luther King Jr., adapted from a speech in St. Louis, MO, "A Realistic Look at the Question of Progress in the Area of Race Relations," on April 10, 1957.

William Douglas is a federal judge in Rio de Janeiro, Brazil, a university professor, a popular speaker, and the author of thirty-five books, including the Brazilian edition of *The 25 Biblical Laws of Success*, with over 250,000 copies sold. He is part of Educafro, a Brazilian organization working to prevent racial prejudice and promote equal opportunities, and is the entrepreneurship coordinator for social projects for United Missions, part of the Brazilian Baptist Convention. He is also part of the Brazilian Evangelical Academy of Writers.

Rubens Teixeira is former CFO of Transpetro, the largest oil and gas company in Brazil, and an analyst for Central Bank of Brazil, as well as a professor, writer, and frequent panelist. He was honored with the National Treasure Prize for his PhD thesis with proposals for the Brazilian economy and is the author of *How to Succeed When You Are Not the Favorite*. He holds a civil engineering degree and a master's degree in nuclear engineering from the Military Institute of Engineering, a law degree and PhD in economics from the Federal University of Brazil (UFF), and a military science degree from the Military Academy of Agulhas Negras. He is also part of the Brazilian Evangelical Academy of Writers.